SHAMBHALA
CLASSICS

Cutting Through Spiritual Materialism

Chögyam Trungpa

Foreword by Sakyong Mipham
Edited by John Baker and Marvin Casper
Illustrated by Glen Eddy

SHAMBHALA
Boston & London
2002

SHAMBHALA PUBLICATIONS, INC.
Horticultural Hall
300 Massachusetts Avenue
Boston, Massachusetts 02115
www.shambhala.com

10 9 8 7 6 5 4 3 2 1

Printed in the United States of America

❀ This edition is printed on acid-free paper that meets
the American National Standards Institute z39.48 Standard.

Distributed in the United States by Random House, Inc.,
and in Canada by Random House of Canada Ltd

LIBRARY OF CONGRESS CATALOGING-IN-PUBLICATION DATA
Trungpa, Chögyam, 1939—
Cutting through spiritual materialism.
Two lecture series given in Boulder, Colo.
1970-71.
Includes index.
1. Spiritual life (Buddhism)   I. Baker, John.
II. Casper, Marvin.   III. Title.
BQ4302.178   1987   294.3′444   87-4619
ISBN 0-87773-050-4
ISBN 1-57062-957-9

To
Chokyi-lodrö the Marpa
Father of the Kagyü lineage

Contents

Foreword   xi

Introduction   3

Spiritual Materialism   13

Surrendering   23

The Guru   31

Initiation   53

Self-Deception   63

The Hard Way   77

The Open Way   91

Sense of Humor   111

The Development of Ego   121

The Six Realms   138

The Four Noble Truths   151

The Bodhisattva Path   167

Shunyata   187

Prajna and Compassion   207

Tantra   217

Index   244

Illustrations

Page 12.   *Senge Dra-dog.* The aspect of Padmasambhava who teaches with the lion's roar that subdues the heretics of hope and fear.

Page 30.   *Marpa.* Father of the Kagyü lineage. Drawn by Sherab Palden Beru.

Page 52.   *Tilopa the Guru.* The teacher of Naropa.

Page 62.   *Pig, Snake and Rooster.* They represent stupidity, aggression, and passion.

Page 76.   *Lohan.* An arhat in meditation posture, a disciple of the Buddha. William Rockhill Nelson Gallery of Art, Kansas City, Mo.

Page 110.   *The Coil of Joy.*

Page 120.   *The Portrait of Samsara.*

Page 150.   *Shakyamuni Buddha in Earth-witness Mudra and Disciples Shariputra and Mahamaudgalyayana.*

Page 166.   *The Three Principle Bodhisattvas—Avalokiteshvara, Manjushri and Vajrapani.* They represent the aspects of the enlightened state—compassion, knowledge and power.

Page 186.   *Prajnaparamita.* The Mother of all the Buddhas, the Ground of all Dharmas.

Page 216.   *Vajradhara and Consort.* The personification of Shakyamuni Buddha teaching Tantra. Symbol of the Absolute in its polarity aspect.

Foreword

The inspiration to find the truth, to see what is real, and to lead a
genuine life—the culmination of which can be enlightenment—is
what underlies every spiritual journey. However, embarking on
this journey is rarely as straightforward as we may wish. The journey toward enlightenment ultimately may be both profound and
simple, yet the process of understanding that simplicity tends to be
multidimensional, if not downright complicated. For in order to
understand a spiritual path, we must acknowledge and understand
our own mind, now, as it pertains to the journey. What misunder-
standings and concepts we may have about a spiritual practice,
we must overcome so that we're not merely practicing according
to our own conceptualized idea. Ego, and the myriad games it
plays to unravel our inspiration for enlightenment, must always be
monitored.

To understand the essential qualities of the spiritual path,
especially what obstacles or conundrums might lie ahead, we need
a clear sense of direction. We need teachings, instructions, and
guidance from someone who has traveled the path and therefore
can give valid and confident advice about how others could travel
this same path. This is what is offered by my father, Chögyam
Trungpa, in *Cutting through Spiritual Materialism*.

These lectures and teachings were given in the early 1970s, at
a crossroads of heightened awareness and spiritual awakening in

the United States. East was beginning to meet West. Having turned away from their parents' values, a whole generation was investigating newly available spiritual paths—many of them quite traditional. People wanted a path that would help them rise above life's mundane trappings to see a more expansive view, a view that would dissolve their feeling of alienation and penetrate life's very meaning. At the same time, many of these seekers were still trying to figure out what a genuine path to liberation was. There was a quality of freshness, exuberance, excitement, and youth, as well as naiveté.

People were naive about the many pitfalls possible on any path. Spiritual awakening is not a happy-go-lucky endeavor. The path of truth is profound—and so are the obstacles and possibilities for self-deception. No matter what the practice or teaching, ego loves to wait in ambush to appropriate spirituality for its own survival and gain. Chögyam Trungpa—who had just arrived in the States from Scotland—tried to clarify these issues. He wanted to raise people's awareness to a level where they could distinguish between what is genuine spiritual progress and what is ego hijacking spirituality for its own purposes. He wanted to help them learn to recognize the grip of the Three Lords of Materialism—strategies that ego can use any time, any place, in order to seduce us from a bigger view back into its self-limiting perspective.

From an early age, Chögyam Trungpa had undergone an arduous education in the monasteries of Kham, on the high plateau of Tibet's eastern region. Even the medieval culture of Tibet was not immune to the perils of spiritual materialism. His teachers had trained him in recognizing the wiliness of ego and in avoiding seduction into seemingly beneficial activities that are really just mundane material pursuits in sacred garments. Here was a teacher who clearly understood the materialistic dilemma of the spiritual path, one who had been steeped and trained in the ancient wisdom of the past—and who could also understand the nuances of modern-day Western-style spiritual blockage. The teachings in this book represent a milestone in the introduction of buddhadharma into American culture.

In part because of the playfulness with which my father taught his young American students, *Cutting Through Spiritual Materialism* has become a classic. For those in the audience who were experimenting with rejecting society in order to pursue an idealistic, transcendental path, his teachings shed new light on working with themselves in the context of their own country, family, and culture. As an enthusiastic newcomer to the West and a spiritual elder as well, he was able to introduce to them the basic workability of their own situation as part of the spiritual path. Rejecting everything was not the solution. Training one's mind, body, and speech in accordance with the truth would bring about the understanding and wisdom that produces peace. Many of those students followed his advice, continuing on their spiritual journeys and at the same time becoming parents, teachers, business people, and even dharma teachers. These people have now become the elders for a new generation of inquisitive minds.

Even though the message of this book was addressed to a particular group at a particular time in history, it is not only for that generation. These teachings will never be dated or pigeonholed. In the last thirty years, in our continuing pursuit of whatever will distract us from the truth of pain and suffering, we have become even more materialistic. In the spiritual realm, there are now even more paths and possibilities to explore than when this book was first published—not just the classic spiritual disciplines, but also many hybrids. This book continues to have the power to sharpen our awareness of spiritual materialism. It deserves our careful attention, as its message is more applicable now than ever.

Sakyong Mipham Rinpoche
October 2001

CUTTING THROUGH
SPIRITUAL MATERIALISM

Introduction

The following series of talks was given in Boulder, Colorado in the fall of 1970 and the spring of 1971. At that time we were just forming Karma Dzong, our meditation center in Boulder. Although most of my students were sincere in their aspiration to walk on the spiritual path, they brought to it a great deal of confusion, misunderstanding and expectation. Therefore, I found it necessary to present to my students an overview of the path and some warnings as to the dangers along that path.

It now seems that publishing these talks may be helpful to those who have become interested in spiritual disciplines. Walking the spiritual path properly is a very subtle process; it is not something to jump into naively. There are numerous sidetracks which lead to a distorted, ego-centered version of spirituality; we can deceive ourselves into thinking we are developing spiritually when instead we are strengthening our egocentricity through spiritual techniques. This fundamental distortion may be referred to as *spiritual materialism.*

These talks first discuss the various ways in which people involve themselves with spiritual materialism, the many forms of self-deception into which aspirants may fall. After this tour of the sidetracks along the way, we discuss the broad outlines of the true spiritual path.

The approach presented here is a classical Buddhist one—not in a formal sense, but in the sense of presenting the heart of the Buddhist approach to spirituality. Although the Buddhist way is not theistic, it does not contradict the theistic disciplines. Rather the differences between the ways are a matter of emphasis and method. The basic problems of spiritual materialism are common to all spiritual disciplines. The Buddhist approach begins with our confusion and suffering and works toward the unraveling of their origin. The theistic approach begins with the richness of God and works toward raising consciousness so as to experience God's presence. But since the obstacles to relating with God are our confusions and negativities, the theistic approach must also deal with them. Spiritual pride, for example, is as much a problem in theistic disciplines as in Buddhism.

According to the Buddhist tradition, the spiritual path is the process of cutting through our confusion, of uncovering the awakened state of mind. When the awakened state of mind is crowded in by ego and its attendant paranoia, it takes on the character of an underlying instinct. So it is not a matter of building up the awakened state of mind, but rather of burning out the confusions which obstruct it. In the process of burning out these confusions, we discover enlightenment. If the process were otherwise, the awakened state of mind would be a product, dependent upon cause and effect and therefore liable to dissolution. Anything which is created must, sooner or later, die. If enlightenment were created in such a way, there would always be the possibility of ego reasserting itself, causing a return to the confused state. Enlightenment is permanent because we have not produced it; we have merely discovered it. In the Buddhist tradition the analogy of the sun appearing from behind the clouds is often used to explain the discovery of enlightenment. In meditation practice we clear away the confusion of ego in order to glimpse the awakened state. The absence of ignorance, of being crowded in, of paranoia, opens up a tremendous view of life. One discovers a different way of being.

The heart of the confusion is that man has a sense of self which seems to him to be continuous and solid. When a thought or emotion or event occurs, there is a sense of someone being conscious of what is happening. You sense that *you* are reading these words. This sense of self is actually a transitory, discontinuous event, which in our confusion seems to be quite solid and continuous. Since we take our confused view as being real, we struggle to maintain and enhance this solid self. We try to feed it pleasures and shield it from pain. Experience continually threatens to reveal our transitoriness to us, so we continually struggle to cover up any possibility of discovering our real condition. "But," we might ask, "if our real condition is an awakened state, why are we so busy trying to avoid becoming aware of it?" It is because we have become so absorbed in our confused view of the world, that we consider it real, the only possible world. This struggle to maintain the sense of a solid, continuous self is the action of ego.

Ego, however, is only partially successful in shielding us from pain. It is the dissatisfaction which accompanies ego's struggle that inspires us to examine what we are doing. Since there are always gaps in our self-consciousness, some insight is possible.

An interesting metaphor used in Tibetan Buddhism to describe the functioning of ego is that of the "Three Lords of Materialism": the "Lord of Form," the "Lord of Speech," and the "Lord of Mind." In the discussion of the Three Lords which follows, the words "materialism" and "neurotic" refer to the action of ego.

The Lord of Form refers to the neurotic pursuit of physical

comfort, security and pleasure. Our highly organized and technological society reflects our preoccupation with manipulating physical surroundings so as to shield ourselves from the irritations of the raw, rugged, unpredictable aspects of life. Push-button elevators, pre-packaged meat, air conditioning, flush toilets, private funerals, retirement programs, mass production, weather satellites, bulldozers, fluorescent lighting, nine-to-five jobs, television—all are attempts to create a manageable, safe, predictable, pleasurable world.

The Lord of Form does not signify the physically rich and secure life-situations we create *per se*. Rather it refers to the neurotic preoccupation that drives us to create them, to try to control nature. It is ego's ambition to secure and entertain itself, trying to avoid all irritation. So we cling to our pleasures and possessions, we fear change or force change, we try to create a nest or playground.

The Lord of Speech refers to the use of intellect in relating to our world. We adopt sets of categories which serve as handles, as ways of managing phenomena. The most fully developed products of this tendency are ideologies, the systems of ideas that rationalize, justify and sanctify our lives. Nationalism, communism, existentialism, Christianity, Buddhism —all provide us with identities, rules of action, and interpretations of how and why things happen as they do.

Again, the use of intellect is not in itself the Lord of Speech. The Lord of Speech refers to the inclination on the part of ego to interpret anything that is threatening or irritating in such a way as to neutralize the threat or turn it into something "positive" from ego's point of view. The Lord of Speech refers to the use of concepts as filters to screen us from a direct perception of what is. The concepts are taken too seriously; they are used as tools to solidify our world and ourselves. If a world of nameable things exists, then "I" as one of the name-able things exists as well. We wish not to leave any room for threatening doubt, uncertainty or confusion.

The Lord of Mind refers to the effort of consciousness to maintain awareness of itself. The Lord of Mind rules when we use spiritual and psychological disciplines as the means of maintaining our self-consciousness, of holding onto our sense of self. Drugs, yoga, prayer, meditation, trances, various psy-chotherapies—all can be used in this way.

Ego is able to convert everything to its own use, even spiri-tuality. For example, if you have learned of a particularly beneficial meditation technique of spiritual practice, then ego's attitude is, first to regard it as an object of fascination and, second to examine it. Finally, since ego is seeming solid and cannot really absorb anything, it can only mimic. Thus ego tries to examine and imitate the practice of meditation and the meditative way of life. When we have learned all the tricks and answers of the spiritual game, we automatically try to imitate spirituality, since real involvement would require the complete elimination of ego, and actually the last thing we want to do is to give up the ego completely. However, we cannot experience that which we are trying to imitate; we can only find some area within the bounds of ego that seems to be the same thing. Ego translates everything in terms of its own state of health, its own inherent qualities. It feels a sense of great accomplishment and excitement at having been able to create such a pattern. At last it has created a tangible ac-complishment, a confirmation of its own individuality.

If we become successful at maintaining our self-conscious-ness through spiritual techniques, then genuine spiritual de-velopment is highly unlikely. Our mental habits become so strong as to be hard to penetrate. We may even go so far as to achieve the totally demonic state of complete "Egohood."

Even though the Lord of Mind is the most powerful in subverting spirituality, still the other two Lords can also rule the spiritual practice. Retreat to nature, isolation, simple, quiet, high people—all can be ways of shielding oneself from irritation, all can be expressions of the Lord of Form. Or perhaps religion may provide us with a rationalization for creating a secure nest, a simple but comfortable home, for acquiring an amiable mate, and a stable, easy job.

The Lord of Speech is involved in spiritual practice as well. In following a spiritual path we may substitute a new religious ideology for our former beliefs, but continue to use it in the old neurotic way. Regardless of how sublime our ideas may be, if we take them too seriously and use them to maintain our ego, we are still being ruled by the Lord of Speech.

Most of us, if we examine our actions, would probably agree that we are ruled by one or more of the Three Lords. "But," we might ask, "so what? This is simply a description of the human condition. Yes, we know that our technology cannot shield us from war, crime, illness, economic insecurity, laborious work, old age and death; nor can our ideologies shield us from doubt, uncertainty, confusion and disorientation; nor can our therapies protect us from the dissolution of the high states of consciousness that we may temporarily achieve and the disillusionment and anguish that follow. But what else are we to do? The Three Lords seem too powerful to overthrow, and we don't know what to replace them with."

The Buddha, troubled by these questions, examined the process by which the Three Lords rule. He questioned why our minds follow them and whether there is another way. He discovered that the Three Lords seduce us by creating a fundamental myth: that we are solid beings. But ultimately the myth is false, a huge hoax, a gigantic fraud, and it is the root of our suffering. In order to make this discovery he had to break through very elaborate defenses erected by the Three Lords to prevent their subjects from discovering the fundamental deception which is the source of their power. We cannot in any way free ourselves from the domination of the Three Lords unless we too cut through, layer by layer, the elaborate defenses of these Lords.

The Lords' defenses are created out of the material of our minds. This material of mind is used by the Lords in such a way as to maintain the basic myth of solidity. In order to see for ourselves how this process works we must examine our own experience. "But how," we might ask, "are we to conduct the examination? What method or tool are we to use?" The method that the Buddha discovered is meditation. He discovered that struggling to find answers did not work. It was only when there were gaps in his struggle that insights came to him. He began to realize that there was a sane, awake quality within him which manifested itself only in the absence of struggle. So the practice of meditation involves "letting be."

There have been a number of misconceptions regarding meditation. Some people regard it as a trancelike state of mind. Others think of it in terms of training, in the sense of mental gymnastics. But meditation is neither of these, although it does involve dealing with neurotic states of mind. The neurotic state of mind is not difficult or impossible to deal with. It has energy, speed and a certain pattern. The practice of meditation involves *letting be*—trying to go with the pattern, trying to go with the energy and the speed. In this way we learn how to deal with these factors, how to relate with them, not in the sense of causing them to mature in the way we would like, but in the sense of knowing them for what they are and working with their pattern.

There is a story regarding the Buddha which recounts how

he once gave teaching to a famous sitar player who wanted to study meditation. The musician asked, "Should I control my mind or should I completely let go?" The Buddha answered, "Since you are a great musician, tell me how you would tune the strings of your instrument." The musician said, "I would make them not too tight and not too loose." "Likewise," said the Buddha, "in your meditation practice you should not impose anything too forcefully on your mind, nor should you let it wander." That is the teaching of letting the mind *be* in a very open way, of feeling the flow of energy without trying to subdue it and without letting it get out of control, of going with the energy pattern of mind. This is meditation practice.

Such practice is necessary generally because our thinking pattern, our conceptualized way of conducting our life in the world, is either too manipulative, imposing itself upon the world, or else runs completely wild and uncontrolled. Therefore, our meditation practice must begin with ego's outermost layer, the discursive thoughts which continually run through our minds, our mental gossip. The Lords use discursive thought as their first line of defense, as the pawns in their effort to deceive us. The more we generate thoughts, the busier we are mentally and the more convinced we are of our existence. So the Lords are constantly trying to activate these thoughts, trying to create a constant overlapping of thoughts so that nothing can be seen beyond them. In true meditation there is no ambition to stir up thoughts, nor is there an ambition to suppress them. They are just allowed to occur spontaneously and become an expression of basic sanity. They become the expression of the precision and the clarity of the awakened state of mind.

If the strategy of continually creating overlapping thoughts is penetrated, then the Lords stir up emotions to distract us.

The exciting, colorful, dramatic quality of the emotions captures our attention as if we were watching an absorbing film show. In the practice of meditation we neither encourage emotions nor repress them. By seeing them clearly, by allowing them to be as they are, we no longer permit them to serve as a means of entertaining and distracting us. Thus they become the inexhaustible energy which fulfills egoless action.

In the absence of thoughts and emotions the Lords bring up a still more powerful weapon, concepts. Labeling phenomena creates a feeling of a solid definite world of "things." Such a solid world reassures us that we are a solid, continuous thing as well. The world exists, therefore I, the perceiver of the world, exist. Meditation involves seeing the transparency of concepts, so that labeling no longer serves as a way of solidifying our world and our image of self. Labeling becomes simply the act of discrimination. The Lords have still further defense mechanisms, but it would be too complicated to discuss them in this context.

By the examination of his own thoughts, emotions, concepts and the other activities of mind, the Buddha discovered that there is no need to struggle to prove our existence, that we need not be subject to the rule of the Three Lords of Materialism. There is no need to struggle to be free; the absence of struggle is in itself freedom. This egoless state is the attainment of Buddhahood. The process of transforming the material of mind from expressions of ego's ambition into expressions of basic sanity and enlightenment through the practice of meditation—this might be said to be the true spiritual path.

Spiritual Materialism

We have come here to learn about spirituality. I trust the genuine quality of this search but we must question its nature. The problem is that ego can convert anything to its own use, even spirituality. Ego is constantly attempting to acquire and apply the teachings of spirituality for its own benefit. The teachings are treated as an external thing, external to "me," a philosophy which we try to imitate. We do not actually want to identify with or become the teachings. So if our teacher speaks of renunciation of ego, we attempt to mimic renunciation of ego. We go through the motions, make the appropriate gestures, but we really do not want to sacrifice any part of our way of life. We become skillful actors, and while playing deaf and dumb to the real meaning of the teachings, we find some comfort in pretending to follow the path.

Whenever we begin to feel any discrepancy or conflict between our actions and the teachings, we immediately interpret the situation in such a way that the conflict is smoothed over. The interpreter is ego in the role of spiritual advisor. The situation is like that of a country where church and state are separate. If the policy of the state is foreign to the teachings of the church, then the automatic reaction of the king is to go to the head of the church, his spiritual advisor. and ask his blessing. The head of the church then works out some justification and gives the policy his blessing under the pretense that the king is the protector of the faith. In an individual's mind, it works out very neatly that way, ego being both king and head of the church.

This rationalization of the spiritual path and one's actions must be cut through if true spirituality is to be realized. However, such rationalizing is not easy to deal with because everything is seen through the filter of ego's philosophy and logic, making all appear neat, precise and very logical. We attempt to find a self-justifying answer for every question. In order to reassure ourselves, we work to fit into our intellectual scheme every aspect of our lives which might be confusing. And our effort is so serious and solemn, so straight-forward and sincere, that it is difficult to be suspicious of it. We always trust the "integrity" of our spiritual advisor.

It does not matter what we use to achieve self-justification: the wisdom of sacred books, diagrams or charts, mathematical calculations, esoteric formulae, fundamentalist religion, depth psychology, or any other mechanism. Whenever we begin to evaluate, deciding that we should or should not do this or that, then we have already associated our practice or our knowledge with categories, one pitted against the other, and that is spiritual materialism, the false spirituality of our spiritual advisor. Whenever we have a dualistic notion such as, "I am doing this because I want to achieve a particular state of consciousness, a particular state of being," then automatically we separate ourselves from the reality of what we are.

If we ask ourselves, "What is wrong with evaluating, with taking sides?", the answer is that, when we formulate a secondary judgment, "I should be doing this and should avoid doing that," then we have achieved a level of complication which takes us a long way from the basic simplicity of what we are. The simplicity of meditation means just experiencing the ape instinct of ego. If anything more than this is laid onto our psychology, then it becomes a very heavy, thick mask, a suit of armor.

It is important to see that the main point of any spiritual practice is to step out of the bureaucracy of ego. This means stepping out of ego's constant desire for a higher, more spiritual, more transcendental version of knowledge, religion, virtue, judgment, comfort or whatever it is that the particular ego is seeking. One must step out of spiritual materialism. If we do not step out of spiritual materialism, if we in fact practice it, then we may eventually find ourselves possessed of a huge collection of spiritual paths. We may feel these spiritual collections to be very precious. We have studied so much. We may have studied Western philosophy or Oriental philosophy, practiced yoga or perhaps have studied under dozens of great masters. We have achieved and we have learned. We believe that we have accumulated a hoard of knowledge. And yet, having gone through all this, there is still something to give up. It is extremely mysterious! How could this happen? Impossible! But unfortunately it is so. Our vast collections of knowledge and experience are just part of ego's display, part of the grandiose quality of ego. We display them to the world and, in so doing, reassure ourselves that we exist, safe and secure, as "spiritual" people.

But we have simply created a shop, an antique shop. We could be specializing in oriental antiques or medieval Christian antiques or antiques from some other civilization or time, but we are, nonetheless, running a shop. Before we filled our shop with so many things the room was beautiful: whitewashed walls and a very simple floor with a bright lamp burning in the ceiling. There was one object of art in the middle of the room and it was beautiful. Everyone who came appreciated its beauty, including ourselves.

But we were not satisfied and we thought, "Since this one object makes my room so beautiful, if I get more antiques, my room will be even more beautiful." So we began to collect, and the end result was chaos.

We searched the world over for beautiful objects—India, Japan, many different countries. And each time we found an antique, because we were dealing with only one object at a time, we saw it as beautiful and thought it would be beautiful in our shop. But when we brought the object home and put it there, it became just another addition to our junky collection. The beauty of the object did not radiate out any more, because it was surrounded by so many other beautiful things. It did not mean anything anymore. Instead of a room full of beautiful antiques we created a junk shop!

Proper shopping does not entail collecting a lot of information or beauty, but it involves fully appreciating each individual object. This is very important. If you really appreciate an object of beauty, then you completely identify with it and forget yourself. It is like seeing a very interesting, fascinating movie and forgetting that you are the audience. At that moment there is no world; your whole being is that scene of that movie. It is that kind of identification, complete involvement with one thing. Did we actually taste it and chew it and swallow it properly, that one object of beauty, that one spiritual teaching? Or did we merely regard it as a part of our vast and growing collection?

I place so much emphasis on this point because I know that all of us have come to the teachings and practice of meditation not to make a lot of money, but because we genuinely want to learn, want to develop ourselves. But, if we regard knowledge as an antique, as "ancient wisdom" to be collected, then we are on the wrong path.

As far as the lineage of teachers is concerned, knowledge is not handed down like an antique. Rather, one teacher experiences the truth of the teachings, and he hands it down as inspiration to his student. That inspiration awakens the student, as his teacher was awakened before him. Then the student hands down the teachings to another student and so the process goes. The teachings are always up to date. They are not "ancient wisdom," an old legend. The teachings are not passed along as information, handed down as a grandfather tells traditional folk tales to his grandchildren. It does not work that way. It is a real experience.

There is a saying in the Tibetan scriptures: "Knowledge must be burned, hammered and beaten like pure gold. Then one can wear it as an ornament." So when you receive spiritual instruction from the hands of another, you do not take it uncritically, but you burn it, you hammer it, you beat it, until the bright, dignified color of gold appears. Then you craft it into an ornament, whatever design you like, and you put it on. Therefore, *dharma* is applicable to every age, to every person; it has a living quality. It is not enough to imitate your master or guru; you are not trying to become a replica of your teacher. The teachings are an individual personal experience, right down to the present holder of the doctrine.

Perhaps many of my readers are familiar with the stories of Naropa and Tilopa and Marpa and Milarepa and Gampopa and the other teachers of the Kagyü lineage. It was a living experience for them, and it is a living experience for the present holders of the lineage. Only the details of their life-situations are different. The teachings have the quality of warm, fresh baked bread; the bread is still warm and hot and fresh. Each baker must apply the general knowledge of how to make bread to his particular dough and oven. Then he must personally experience the freshness of this bread and must cut it fresh and eat it warm. He must make the teachings his own and then must practice them. It is a very living process. There is no deception in terms of collecting knowledge. We must work with our individual experiences. When we become confused, we cannot turn back to our collection of knowledge and try to find some confirmation or consolation: "The teacher and the whole teaching is on my side." The spiritual path does not go that way. It is a lonely, individual path.

Q: Do you think spiritual materialism is a particularly American problem?
A: Whenever teachings come to a country from abroad, the problem of spiritual materialism is intensified. At the moment America is, without any doubt, fertile ground ready for the teachings. And because America is so fertile, seeking spirituality, it is possible for America to inspire charlatans. Charlatans would not choose to be charlatans unless they were inspired to do so. Otherwise, they would be bank robbers or bandits, inasmuch as they want to make money and become famous. Because America is looking so hard for spirituality, religion becomes an easy way to make money and achieve fame. So we see charlatans in the role of student, *chela*, as well as in the role of guru. I think America at this particular time is a very interesting ground.

Q: Have you accepted any spiritual master as a guru, any particular living spiritual master?
A: At present there is no one. I left my gurus and teachers

behind in Tibet, physically, but the teachings stay with me and continue.

Q: So who are you following, more or less?
A: Situations are the voice of my guru, the presence of my guru.

Q: After Shakyamuni Buddha attained enlightenment, was there some trace of ego left in him so that he could carry on his teachings?
A: The teaching just happened. He did not have the desire to teach or not to teach. He spent seven weeks sitting under the shade of a tree and walking along the bank of a river. Then someone just happened along and he began to speak. One has no choice; you are there, an open person. Then the situation presents itself and teaching happens. That is what is called "Buddha activity."

Q: It is difficult not to be acquisitive about spirituality. Is this desire for acquisitions something that is shed along the way?
A: You should let the first impulse die down. Your first impulse towards spirituality might put you into some particular spiritual scene; but if you work with that impulse, then the impulse gradually dies down and at some stage becomes tedious, monotonous. This is a useful message. You see, it is essential to relate to yourself, to your own experience, *really*. If one does not relate to oneself, then the spiritual path becomes dangerous, becomes purely external entertainment, rather than an organic personal experience.

Q: If you decide to seek your way out of ignorance, you can almost definitely assume that anything you do that feels good will be beneficial to the ego and actually blocking the path. Anything that seems right to you will be wrong, anything that doesn't turn you upside-down will bury you. Is there any way out of this?

A: If you perform some act which is seemingly right, it does not mean that it is wrong, for the very reason that wrong and right are out of the picture altogether. You are not working on any side, neither the "good" side nor the "bad" side, but you are working with the totality of the whole, beyond "this" and "that." I would say there is complete action. There is no partial act, but whatever we do in connection with good and bad seems to be a partial act.

Q: If you are feeling very confused and trying to work your way out of the confusion, it would seem that you are trying too hard. But if you do not try at all, then are we to understand that we are fooling ourselves?

A: Yes, but that does not mean that one has to live by the extremes of trying too hard or not trying at all. One has to work with a kind of "middle way," a complete state of "being as you are." We could describe this with a lot of words, but one really has to do it. If you really start living the middle way, then you will see it, you will find it. You must allow yourself to trust yourself, to trust in your own intelligence. We are tremendous people, we have tremendous things in us. We simply have to let ourselves be. External aid cannot help. If you are not willing to let yourself grow, then you fall into the self-destructive process of confusion. It is self-destruction rather than destruction by someone else. That is why it is effective; because it is *self*-destruction.

Q: What is faith? Is it useful?

A: Faith could be simple-minded, trusting, blind faith, or it could be definite confidence which cannot be destroyed. Blind faith has no inspiration. It is very naive. It is not creative, though not exactly destructive. It is not creative because your faith and yourself have never made any connection, any communication. You just blindly accepted the whole belief, very naively.

In the case of faith as confidence, there is a living reason to be confident. You do not expect that there will be a pre-fabricated solution mysteriously presented to you. You work with existing situations without fear, without any doubt about involving yourself. This approach is extremely creative and positive. If you have definite confidence, you are so sure of yourself that you do not have to check yourself. It is *absolute* confidence, real understanding of what is going on now, therefore you do not hesitate to follow other paths or deal in whatever way is necessary with each new situation.

Q: What guides you on the path?
A: Actually, there does not seem to be any particular guidance. In fact, if someone is guiding you, that is suspicious, because you are relying on something external. Being fully what you are in yourself becomes guidance, but not in the sense of vanguard, because you do not have a guide to follow. You do not have to follow someone's tail, but you sail along. In other words, the guide does not walk ahead of you, but walks with you.

Q: Could you say something more about the way in which meditation short-circuits the protective mechanisms of the ego?
A: The protective mechanism of ego involves checking oneself, which is an unnecessary kind of self-observance. Meditation is not based on meditating *on* a particular subject by checking oneself; but meditation is complete indentification

with whatever techniques you are employing. Therefore there will be no effort to secure oneself in the practice of meditation.

Q: I seem to be living in a spiritual junkyard. How can I make it into a simple room with one beautiful object?

A: In order to develop an appreciation of your collection you have to start with one item. One has to find a stepping stone, a source of inspiration. Perhaps you would not have to go through the rest of the items in your collection if you studied just one piece of material. That one piece of material could be a sign-post that you managed to confiscate in New York City, it could be as insignificant as that. But one must start with one thing, see its simplicity, the rugged quality of this piece of junk or this beautiful antique. If we could manage to start with just one thing, then that would be the equivalent of having one object in an empty room. I think it is a question of finding a stepping stone. Because we have so many possessions in our collection, a large part of the problem is that we do not know where to begin. One has to allow one's instinct to determine which will be the first thing to pick up.

Q: Why do you think that people are so protective of their egos? Why is it so hard to let go of one's ego?

A: People are afraid of the emptiness of space, or the absence of company, the absence of a shadow. It could be a terrifying experience to have no one to relate to, nothing to relate with. The idea of it can be extremely frightening, though not the real experience. It is generally a fear of space, a fear that we will not be able to anchor ourselves to any solid ground, that we will lose our identity as a fixed and solid and definite thing. This could be very threatening.

Surrendering

At this point we may have come to the conclusion that we should drop the whole game of spiritual materialism; that is, we should give up trying to defend and improve ourselves. We may have glimpsed that our struggle is futile and may wish to surrender, to completely abandon our efforts to defend ourselves. But how many of us could actually do this? It is not as simple and easy as we might think. To what degree could we really let go and be open? At what point would we become defensive?

In this lecture we will discuss surrendering, particularly in terms of the relationship between work on the neurotic state of mind and work with a personal guru or teacher. Surrendering to the "guru" could mean opening our minds to life-situations as well as to an individual teacher. However, if our life-style and inspiration is working toward an unfolding of the mind, then we will almost certainly find a personal guru as well. So in the next few talks we will emphasize relating to a personal teacher.

One of the difficulties in surrendering to a guru is our preconceptions regarding him and our expectations of what will happen with him. We are preoccupied with ideas of what we would like to experience with our teacher: "I would like to see this; that would be the best way to see it; I would like to experience this particular situation, because it is in exact accordance with my expectation and fascination."

So we try to fit things into pigeonholes, try to fit the situation to our expectations, and we cannot surrender any part of our anticipation to all. If we search for a guru or teacher, we expect him to be saintly, peaceful, quiet, a simple and yet wise man. When we find that he does not match our expectations, then we begin to be disappointed, we begin to doubt.

In order to establish a real teacher-student relationship it is necessary for us to give up all our preconceptions regarding that relationship and the condition of opening and surrender. "Surrender" means opening oneself completely, trying to get beyond fascination and expectation.

Surrender also means acknowledging the raw, rugged, clumsy and shocking qualities of one's ego, acknowledging them and surrendering them as well. Generally, we find it very difficult to give out and surrender our raw and rugged qualities of ego. Although we may hate ourselves, at the same time we find our self-hatred a kind of occupation. In spite of the fact that we may dislike what we are and find that self-condemnation painful, still we cannot give it up completely. If we begin to give up our self-criticism, then we may feel that we are losing our occupation, as though someone were taking away our job. We would have no further occupation if we were to surrender everything; there would be nothing to hold on to. Self-evaluation and self-criticism are, basically, neurotic tendencies which derive from our not having enough confidence in ourselves, "confidence" in the sense of seeing what we are, knowing what we are, knowing that we can afford to open. We *can* afford to surrender that raw and rugged neurotic quality of self and step out of fascination, step out of preconceived ideas.

We must surrender our hopes and expectations, as well as our fears, and march directly into disappointment, work with disappointment, go into it and make it our way of life, which is a very hard thing to do. Disappointment is a good sign of basic intelligence. It cannot be compared to anything else: it is so sharp, precise, obvious and direct. If we can open, then we suddenly begin to see that our expectations are irrelevant compared with the reality of the situations we are facing. This automatically brings a feeling of disappointment.

Disappointment is the best chariot to use on the path of the dharma. It does not confirm the existence of our ego and its dreams. However, if we are involved with spiritual materialism, if we regard spirituality as a part of our accumulation of learning and virtue, if spirituality becomes a way of building ourselves up, then of course the whole process of surrendering is completely distorted. If we regard spirituality as a way of making ourselves comfortable, then whenever we experience something unpleasant, a disappointment, we try to rationalize it: "Of course this must be an act of wisdom on the part of the guru, because I know, I'm quite certain the guru doesn't do harmful things. Guruji is a perfect being and whatever Guruji does is right. Whatever Guruji does is for me, because he is on my side. So I can afford to open. I can safely surrender. I know that I am treading on the right path." Something is not quite right about such an attitude. It is, at best, simple-minded and naive. We are captivated by the awesome, inspiring, dignified and colorful aspect of "Guruji." We dare not contemplate any other way. We develop the conviction that whatever we experience is part of our spiritual development. "I've made it, I have experienced it, I am a self-made person and I know everything, roughly, because I've read books and they confirm my beliefs, my rightness, my ideas. Everything coincides."

We can hold back in still another way, not really surrendering because we feel that we are very genteel, sophisticated and dignified people. "Surely we can't give ourselves to this dirty, ordinary street-scene of reality." We have the feeling that every step of the path we tread should be a lotus petal and we develop a logic that interprets whatever happens to us accordingly. If we fall, we create a soft landing which prevents sudden shock. Surrendering does not involve preparing for a soft landing; it means just landing on hard, ordinary ground, on rocky, wild countryside. Once we open ourselves, then we land on *what is*.

Traditionally, surrendering is symbolized by such practices as prostration, which is the act of falling on the ground in a gesture of surrender. At the same time we open psychologically and surrender completely by identifying ourselves with the lowest of the low, acknowledging our raw and rugged quality. There is nothing that we fear to lose once we identify ourselves with the lowest of the low. By doing so, we prepare ourselves to be an empty vessel, ready to receive the teachings.

In the Buddhist tradition, there is this basic formula: "I take refuge in the Buddha, I take refuge in the dharma, I take refuge in the sangha." I take refuge in the Buddha as the example of surrender, the example of acknowledging negativity as a part of our makeup and opening to it. I take refuge in the dharma—dharma, the "law of existence," life as it is. I am willing to open my eyes to the circumstances of life as they are. I am not willing to view them as spiritual or mystical, but I am willing to see the situations of life as they really are.

I take refuge in the sangha. "Sangha" means "community of people on the spiritual path," "companions." I am willing to share my experience of the whole environment of life with my fellow pilgrims, my fellow searchers, those who walk with me; but I am not willing to lean on them in order to gain support. I am only willing to walk along with them. There is a very dangerous tendency to lean on one another as we tread the path. If a group of people leans one upon the other, then if one should happen to fall down, everyone falls down. So we do not lean on anyone else. We just walk with each other, side by side, shoulder to shoulder, working with each other, going with each other. This approach to surrendering, this idea of taking refuge is very profound.

The wrong way to take refuge involves seeking shelter— worshipping mountains, sun gods, moon gods, deities of any kind simply because they would seem to be greater than we. This kind of refuge-taking is similar to the response of the little child who says, "If you beat me, I'll tell my mommy," thinking that his mother is a great, archetypically powerful person. If he is attacked, his automatic recourse is to his mother, an invincible and all-knowing, all-powerful personality. The child believes his mother can protect him, in fact that she is the only person who can save him. Taking refuge in a mother or father-principle is truly self-defeating; the refuge-seeker has no real basic strength at all, no true inspiration. He is constantly busy assessing greater and smaller powers. If we are small, then someone greater can crush us. We seek refuge because we cannot afford to be small and without protection. We tend to be apologetic: "I am such a small thing, but I acknowledge your great quality. I would like to worship and join your greatness, so will you please protect me?"

Surrendering is not a question of being low and stupid, nor of wanting to be elevated and profound. It has nothing to do with levels and evaluation. Instead, we surrender because we would like to communicate with the world "as it is." We do not have to classify ourselves as learners or ignorant people. We know where we stand, therefore we make the gesture of surrendering, of opening, which means communication, link, direct communication with the object of our surrendering. We are not embarrassed about our rich collection of raw, rugged, beautiful and clean qualities. We present everything to the object of our surrendering. The basic act of surrender does not involve the worship of an external power. Rather it means working together with inspiration, so that one becomes an open vessel into which knowledge can be poured.

Thus openness and surrendering are the necessary preparation for working with a spiritual friend. We acknowledge our fundamental richness rather than bemoan the imagined poverty of our being. We know we are worthy to receive the teachings, worthy of relating ourselves to the wealth of the opportunities for learning.

The Guru

Coming to the study of spirituality we are faced with the problem of our relationship with a teacher, lama, guru, whatever we call the person we suppose will give us spiritual understanding. These words, especially the term "guru," have acquired meanings and associations in the West which are misleading and which generally add to the confusion around the issue of what it means to study with a spiritual teacher. This is not to say that people in the East understand how to relate to a guru while Westerners do not; the problem is universal. People always come to the study of spirituality with some ideas already fixed in their minds of what it is they are going to get and how to deal with the person from whom they think they will get it. The very notion that we will *get* something from a guru—happiness, peace of mind, wisdom, whatever it is we seek—is one of the most difficult preconceptions of all. So I think it would be helpful to examine the way in which some famous students dealt with the problems of how to relate to spirituality and a spiritual teacher. Perhaps these examples will have some relevance for our own individual search.

One of the most renowned Tibetan masters and also one of the main gurus of the Kagyü lineage, of which I am a member, was Marpa, student of the Indian teacher Naropa and guru to Milarepa, his most famous spiritual son. Marpa is an example of someone who was on his way to becoming a successful self-made man. He was born into a farming family, but as a youth he became ambitious and chose scholarship and the priesthood as his route to prominence. We can imagine what tremendous effort and determination it must have taken for the son of a farmer to raise himself to the position of priest in his local religious tradition. There were only a few ways for such a man to achieve any kind of position in 10th century Tibet—as a merchant, a bandit, or especially as a priest. Joining the local clergy at that time was roughly equivalent to becoming a doctor, lawyer and college professor, all rolled into one.

Marpa began by studying Tibetan, Sanskrit, several other languages and the spoken language of India. After about three years of such study he was proficient enough to begin earning money as a scholar, and with this money he financed his religious study, eventually becoming a Buddhist priest of sorts. Such a position brought with it a certain degree of local prominence, but Marpa was more ambitious and so, although he was married by now and had a family, he continued to save his earnings until he had amassed a large amount of gold.

At this point Marpa announced to his relatives his intentions to travel to India to collect more teachings. India at this time was the world center for Buddhist studies, home of Nalanda University and the greatest Buddhist sages and scholars. It was Marpa's intention to study and collect texts unknown in Tibet, bring them home and translate them, thus establishing himself as a great scholar-translator. The journey to India was at that time and until fairly recently a long and dangerous one, and Marpa's family and elders tried to dissuade him from it. But he was determined and so set out accompanied by a friend and fellow scholar.

After a difficult journey of some months they crossed the Himalayas into India and proceeded to Bengal where they went their separate ways. Both men were well qualified in the study of language and religion, and so they decided to search for their own teachers, to suit their own tastes. Before parting they agreed to meet again for the journey home.

While he was travelling through Nepal, Marpa had happened to hear of the teacher Naropa, a man of enormous fame. Naropa had been abbot of Nalanda University, perhaps the greatest center for Buddhist studies the world has ever known. At the height of his career, feeling that he understood the sense but not the real meaning of the teachings, he abandoned his post and set out in search of a guru. For twelve years he endured terrific hardship at the hands of his teacher Tilopa, until finally he achieved realization. By the time Marpa heard of him, he was reputed to be one of the greatest Buddhist saints ever to have lived. Naturally Marpa set out to find him.

Eventually Marpa found Naropa living in poverty in a simple house in the forests of Bengal. He had expected to find so great a teacher living in the midst of a highly evolved religious setting of some sort, and so he was somewhat disappointed. However, he was a bit confused by the strangeness of a foreign country and willing to make some allowances, thinking that perhaps this was the way Indian teachers lived. Also, his appreciation of Naropa's fame outweighed his disappointment, and so he gave Naropa most of his gold and asked for teachings. He explained that he was a married man, a priest, scholar and farmer from Tibet, and that he was not willing to give up this life he had made for himself, but that he wanted to collect teachings to take back to Tibet to translate in order to earn more money. Naropa agreed to Marpa's requests quite easily, gave Marpa instruction, and everything went smoothly.

After some time Marpa decided that he had collected enough teachings to suit his purposes and prepared to return home. He proceeded to an inn in a large town where he rejoined his travelling companion, and the two sat down to compare the results of their efforts. When his friend saw what Marpa had collected, he laughed and said, "What you have here is worthless! We already have those teachings in Tibet. You must have found something more exciting and rare. I found fantastic teachings which I received from very great masters."

Marpa, of course, was extremely frustrated and upset, having come such a long way and with so much difficulty and expense, so he decided to return to Naropa and try once more. When he arrived at Naropa's hut and asked for more rare and exotic and advanced teachings, to his surprise Naropa told him, "I'm sorry, but you can't receive these teachings from me. You will have to go and receive these from someone else, a man named Kukuripa. The journey is difficult, especially so because Kukuripa lives on an island in the middle of a lake of poison. But he is the one you will have to see if you want these teachings."

By this time Marpa was becoming desperate, so he decided to try the journey. Besides, if Kukuripa had teachings which even the great Naropa could not give him and, in addition, lived in the middle of a poisonous lake, then he must be quite an extraordinary teacher, a great mystic.

So Marpa made the journey and managed to cross the lake to the island where he began to look for Kukuripa. There he found an old Indian man living in filth in the midst of hundreds of female dogs. The situation was outlandish, to say the least, but Marpa nevertheless tried to speak to Kukuripa. All he got was gibberish. Kukuripa seemed to be speaking complete nonsense.

Now the situation was almost unbearable. Not only was Kukuripa's speech completely unintelligible, but Marpa had to constantly be on guard against the hundreds of bitches. As soon as he was able to make a relationship with one dog, another would bark and threaten to bite him. Finally, almost beside himself, Marpa gave up altogether, gave up trying to take notes, gave up trying to receive any kind of secret doctrine. And at that point Kukuripa began to speak to him in a totally intelligible, coherent voice and the dogs stopped harrassing him and Marpa received the teachings.

After Marpa had finished studying with Kukuripa, he returned once more to his original guru, Naropa. Naropa told him, "Now you must return to Tibet and teach. It isn't enough to receive the teachings in a theoretical way. You must go through certain life experiences. Then you can come back again and study further."

Once more Marpa met his fellow searcher and together they began the long journey back to Tibet. Marpa's companion had also studied a great deal and both men had stacks of manuscripts and, as they proceeded, they discussed what they had learned. Soon Marpa began to feel uneasy about his friend, who seemed more and more inquisitive to discover what teachings Marpa had collected. Their conversations together seemed to turn increasingly around this subject, until finally his travelling companion decided that Marpa had obtained more valuable teachings than himself, and so he became quite jealous. As they were crossing a river in a ferry, Marpa's colleague began to complain of being uncomfortable and crowded by all the baggage they were carrying. He shifted his position in the boat, as if to make himself more comfortable, and in so doing managed to throw all of Marpa's manuscripts into the river. Marpa tried desperately to rescue them, but they were gone. All the texts he had gone to such lengths to collect had disappeared in an instant.

So it was with a feeling of great loss that Marpa returned to Tibet. He had many stories to tell of his travels and studies, but he had nothing solid to prove his knowledge and experience. Nevertheless, he spent several years working and teaching until, to his surprise, he began to realize that his writings would have been useless to him, even had he been able to save them. While he was in India he had only taken written notes on those parts of the teachings he had not understood. He had not written down those teachings which were part of his own experience. It was only years later that he discovered that they had actually become a part of him.

With this discovery Marpa lost all desire to profit from the teachings. He was no longer concerned with making money or achieving prestige but instead was inspired to realize enlightenment. So he collected gold dust as an offering to Naropa and once again made the journey to India. This time he went full of longing to see his guru and desire for the teachings.

However, Marpa's next encounter with Naropa was quite different than before. Naropa seemed very cold and impersonal, almost hostile, and his first words to Marpa were, "Good to see you again. How much gold have you for my teachings?" Marpa had brought a large amount of gold but wanted to save some for his expenses and the trip home, so he opened his pack and gave Naropa only a portion of what he had. Naropa looked at the offering and said, "No, this is not enough. I need more gold than this for my teaching. Give me all your gold." Marpa gave him a bit more and still Naropa demanded all, and this went on until finally Naropa laughed and said, "Do you think you can buy my teaching with your deception?" At this point Marpa yielded and gave Naropa all the gold he had. To his shock, Naropa picked up the bags and began flinging the gold dust in the air.

Suddenly Marpa felt extremely confused and paranoid. He could not understand what was happening. He had worked hard for the gold to buy the teaching he so wanted. Naropa had seemed to indicate that he needed the gold and would teach Marpa in return for it. Yet he was throwing it away! Then Naropa said to him, "What need have I of gold? The whole world is gold for me!"

This was a great moment of opening for Marpa. He opened and was able to receive teaching. He stayed with Naropa for a long time after that and his training was quite austere, but he did not simply listen to the teachings as before; he had to work his way through them. He had to give up everything he had, not just his material possessions, but whatever he was holding back in his mind had to go. It was a continual process of opening and surrender.

In Milarepa's case, the situation developed quite differently. He was a peasant, much less learned and sophisticated than Marpa had been when he met Naropa, and he had committed many crimes including murder. He was miserably unhappy, yearned for enlightenment, and was willing to pay any fee that Marpa might ask. So Marpa had Milarepa pay on a very literal physical level. He had him build a series of houses for him, one after the other, and after each was completed Marpa would tell Milarepa to tear the house down and put all the stones back where he had found them, so as not to mar the landscape. Each time Marpa ordered Milarepa to dismantle a house, he would give some absurd excuse, such as having been drunk when he ordered the house built or never having ordered such a house at all. And each time Milarepa, full of longing for the teachings, would tear the house down and start again.

Finally Marpa designed a tower with nine stories. Milarepa suffered terrific physical hardship in carrying the stones and building the house and, when he had finished, he went to Marpa and once more asked for the teachings. But Marpa said to him, "You want to receive teachings from me, just like that, merely because you built this tower for me? Well, I'm afraid you will still have to give me a gift as an initiation fee."

By this time Milarepa had no possessions left whatsoever, having spent all his time and labor building towers. But Damema, Marpa's wife, felt sorry for him and said, "These towers you have built are such a wonderful gesture of devotion and faith. Surely my husband won't mind if I give you some sacks of barley and a roll of cloth for your initiation fee." So Milarepa took the barley and cloth to the initiation circle where Marpa was teaching and offered them as his fee, along with the gifts of the other students. But Marpa, when he recognized the gift, was furious and shouted at Milarepa, "These things belong to me, you hypocrite! You try to deceive me!" And he literally kicked Milarepa out of the initiation circle.

At this point Milarepa gave up all hope of ever getting Marpa to give him the teachings. In despair, he decided to commit suicide and was just about to kill himself when Marpa came to him and told him that he was ready to receive the teaching.

The process of receiving teaching depends upon the student

giving something in return; some kind of psychological surrender is necessary, a gift of some sort. This is why we must
discuss surrendering, opening, giving up expectations, before
we can speak of the relationship between teacher and student.
It is essential to surrender, to open yourself, to present whatever you are to the guru, rather than trying to present yourself
as a worthwhile student. It does not matter how much you are
willing to pay, how correctly you behave, how clever you are
at saying the right thing to your teacher. It is not like having
an interview for a job or buying a new car. Whether or not
you will get the job depends upon your credentials, how well
you are dressed, how beautifully your shoes are polished, how
well you speak, how good your manners are. If you are buying a car, it is a matter of how much money you have and
how good your credit is.

But when it comes to spirituality, something more is required. It is not a matter of applying for a job, of dressing up
to impress our potential employer. Such deception does not
apply to an interview with a guru, because he sees right
through us. He is amused if we dress up especially for the
interview. Making ingratiating gestures is not applicable in
this situation; in fact it is futile. We must make a real commitment to being open with our teacher; we must be willing
to give up all our preconceptions. Milarepa expected Marpa
to be a great scholar and a saintly person, dressed in yogic
costume with beads, reciting mantras, meditating. Instead he
found Marpa working on his farm, directing the laborers and
plowing his land.

I am afraid the word "guru" is overused in the West. It
would be better to speak of one's "spiritual friend," because
the teachings emphasize a mutual meeting of two minds. It
is a matter of mutual communication, rather than a master-

servant relationship between a highly evolved being and a miserable, confused one. In the master-servant relationship the highly evolved being may appear not even to be sitting on his seat but may seem to be floating, levitating, looking down at us. His voice is penetrating, pervading space. Every word, every cough, every movement that he makes is a gesture of wisdom. But this is a dream. A guru should be a spiritual friend who communicates and presents his qualities to us, as Marpa did with Milarepa and Naropa with Marpa. Marpa presented his quality of being a farmer-yogi. He happened to have seven children and a wife, and he looked after his farm, cultivating the land and supporting himself and his family. But these activities were just an ordinary part of his life. He cared for his students as he cared for his crops and family. He was so thorough, paying attention to every detail of his life, that he was able to be a competent teacher as well as a competent father and farmer. There was no physical or spiritual materialism in Marpa's life-style at all. He did not emphasize spirituality and ignore his family or his physical relationship to the earth. If you are not involved with materialism, either spiritually or physically, then there is no emphasis made on any extreme.

Nor is it helpful to choose someone for your guru simply because he is famous, someone who is renowned for having published stacks of books and converted thousands or millions of people. Instead the guideline is whether or not you are able actually to communicate with the person, directly and thoroughly. How much self-deception are you involved in? If you really open yourself to your spiritual friend, then you are bound to work together. Are you able to talk to him thoroughly and properly? Does he know anything about you? Does he know anything about himself, for that matter? Is the guru really able to see through your masks, communicate with you properly, directly? In searching for a teacher, this seems to be the guideline rather than fame or wisdom.

There is an interesting story of a group of people who decided to go and study under a great Tibetan teacher. They had already studied somewhat with other teachers, but had decide to concentrate on trying to learn from this particular person. They were all very anxious to become his students and so sought an audience with him, but this great teacher would not accept any of them. "Under one condition only will I accept you," he said. "If you are willing to renounce your previous teachers." They all pleaded with him, telling him how much they were devoted to him, how great his reputation was, and how much they would like to study with him. But he would not accept any of them unless they would meet his condition. Finally all except one person in the party decided to renounce their previous teachers, from whom they had in fact learned a great deal. The guru seemed to be quite happy when they did so and told them all to come back the next day. But when they returned he said to them, "I understand your hypocrisy. The next time you go to another teacher you will renounce me. So get out." And he chased them all out except for the one person who valued what he had learned previously. The person he accepted was not willing to play any more lying games, was not willing to try to please a guru by pretending to be different from what he was. If you are going to make friends with a spiritual master, you must make friends simply, openly, so that the communication takes place between equals, rather than trying to win the master over to you.

In order to be accepted by your guru as a friend, you have to open yourself completely. And in order that you might open, you will probably have to undergo tests by your spiritual

friend and by life situations in general, all of these tests taking
the form of disappointment. At some stage you will doubt that
your spiritual friend has any feeling, any emotion toward you
at all. This is dealing with your own hypocrisy. The hypocrisy,
the pretense and basic twist of ego, is extremely hard; it has
a very thick skin. We tend to wear suits of armor, one over
the other. This hypocrisy is so dense and multi-levelled that,
as soon as we remove one layer of our suit of armor, we find
another beneath it. We hope we will not have to completely
undress. We hope that stripping off only a few layers will
make us presentable. Then we appear in our new suit of armor
with such an ingratiating face, but our spiritual friend does
not wear any armor at all; he is a naked person. Compared
with his nakedness, we are wearing cement. Our armor is so
thick that our friend cannot feel the texture of our skin, our
bodies. He cannot even see our faces properly. There are
many stories of teacher-student relationships in the past in
which the student had to make long journeys and endure many
hardships until his fascination and impulses began to wear
out. This seems to be the point: the impulse of searching for
something is, in itself, a hang-up. When this impulse begins
to wear out, then our fundamental basic nakedness begins to
appear and the meeting of the two minds begins to take place.

It has been said that the first stage of meeting one's spiritual friend is like going to a supermarket. You are excited
and you dream of all the different things that you are going
to buy: the richness of your spiritual friend and the colorful
qualities of his personality. The second stage of your relationship is like going to court, as though you were a criminal.
You are not able to meet your friend's demands and you
begin to feel self-conscious, because you know that he knows

as much as you know about yourself, which is extremely embarrassing. In the third stage when you go to see your spiritual friend, it is like seeing a cow happily grazing in a meadow. You just admire its peacefulness and the landscape and then you pass on. Finally the fourth stage with one's spiritual friend is like passing a rock in the road. You do not even pay attention to it; you just pass by and walk away.

At the beginning a kind of courtship with the guru is taking place, a love affair. How much are you able to win this person over to you? There is a tendency to want to be closer to your spiritual friend, because you really want to learn. You feel such admiration for him. But at the same time he is very frightening; he puts you off. Either the situation does not coincide with your expectations or there is a self-conscious feeling that "I may not be able to open completely and thoroughly." A love-hate relationship, a kind of surrendering and running away process develops. In other words, we begin to play a game, a game of wanting to open, wanting to be involved in a love affair with our guru, and then wanting to run away from him. If we get too close to our spiritual friend, then we begin to feel overpowered by him. As it says in the old Tibetan proverb: "A guru is like a fire. If you get too close you get burned; if you stay too far away you don't get enough heat." This kind of courtship takes place on the part of the student. You tend to get too close to the teacher, but once you do, you get burned. Then you want to run away altogether.

Eventually the relationship begins to become very substantial and solid. You begin to realize that wanting to be near and wanting to be far away from the guru is simply your own game. It has nothing to do with the real situation, but is just your own hallucination. The guru or spiritual friend is always there burning, always a life-fire. You can play games with him or not, as you choose.

Then the relationship with one's spiritual friend begins to become very creative. You accept the situations of being overwhelmed by him and distant from him. If he decides to play the role of cold icy water, you accept it. If he decides to play the role of hot fire, you accept it. Nothing can shake you at all and you come to a reconciliation with him.

The next stage is that, having accepted everything your spiritual friend might do, you begin to lose your own inspiration because you have completely surrendered, completely given up. You feel yourself reduced to a speck of dust. You are insignificant. You begin to feel that the only world that exists is that of this spiritual friend, the guru. It is as though you were watching a fascinating movie; the movie is so exciting that you become part of it. There is no you and no cinema hall, no chairs, no people watching, no friends sitting next to you. The movie is all that exists. This is called the "honeymoon period" in which everything is seen as a part of this central being, the guru. You are just a useless, insignificant person who is continuously being fed by this great, fascinating central being. Whenever you feel weak or tired or bored, you go and just sit in the cinema hall and are entertained, uplifted, rejuvenated. At this point the phenomenon of the personality cult becomes prominent. The guru is the only person in the world who exists, alive and vibrant. The very meaning of your life depends upon him. If you die, you die for him. If you live, you survive for him and are insignificant.

However, this love affair with your spiritual friend cannot last forever. Sooner or later its intensity must wane and you must face your own life-situation and your own psychology. It is like having married and finished the honeymoon. You not only feel conscious of your lover as the central focus of your attention, but you begin to notice his or her life-style as well. You begin to notice what it is that makes this person a teacher, beyond the limits of his individuality and personality. Thus the principle of the "universality of the guru" comes into the picture as well. Every problem you face in life is a part of your marriage. Whenever you experience difficulties, you hear the words of the guru. This is the point at which one begins to gain one's independence from the guru as lover, because every situation becomes an expression of the teachings. First you surrendered to your spiritual friend. Then you communicated and played games with him. And now you have come to the state of complete openness. As a result of this openness you begin to see the guru-quality in every life-situation, that all situations in life offer you the opportunity to be as open as you are with the guru, and so all things can become the guru.

Milarepa had a vivid vision of his guru Marpa while he was meditating in very strict retreat in Red Rock Jewel Valley. Weak with hunger and battered by the elements, he had fainted while trying to collect firewood outside his cave. When he regained consciousness, he looked to the east and saw white clouds in the direction where Marpa lived. With great longing he sang a song of supplication, telling Marpa how much he longed to be with him. Then Marpa appeared in a vision, riding a white snow lion, and said to him something like, "What is the matter with you? Have you had a neurotic upheaval of some sort? You understand the dharma, so continue to practice meditation." Milarepa took comfort and returned to his cave to meditate. His reliance and dependence upon Marpa at this point indicates that he had not yet freed himself from the notion of guru as personal, individual friend.

However, when Milarepa returned to his cave, he found it full of demons with eyes as big as saucepans and bodies the size of thumbs. He tried all kinds of ploys to get them to stop mocking and tormenting him, but they would not leave until Milarepa finally stopped trying to play games, until he recognized his own hypocrisy and gave in to openness. From this point on you see a tremendous change of style in Milarepa's songs, because he had learned to identify with the universal quality of guru, rather than solely relating to Marpa as an individual person.

The spiritual friend becomes part of you, as well as being an individual, external person. As such the guru, both internal and external, plays a very important part in penetrating and exposing our hypocrisies. The guru can be a person who acts as a mirror, reflecting you, or else your own basic intelligence takes the form of the spiritual friend. When the internal guru begins to function, then you can never escape the demand to open. The basic intelligence follows you everywhere; you cannot escape your own shadow. "Big Brother is watching you." Though it is not external entities who are watching us and haunting us; we haunt ourselves. Our own shadow is watching us.

We could look at it in two different ways. We could see the guru as a ghost, haunting and mocking us for our hypocrisy. There could be a demonic quality in realizing what we are. And yet there is always the creative quality of the spiritual friend which also becomes a part of us. The basic intelligence is continuously present in the situations of life. It is so sharp and penetrating that at some stage, even if you want to get rid of it, you cannot. Sometimes it has a stern expression, sometimes an inspiring smile. It has been said in the Tantric tradition that you do not see the face of the guru, but you see the expression of his face all the time. Either smiling, grinning, or frowning angrily, it is part of every life-situation. The basic intelligence, *tathagata-garbha*, Buddha-nature, is always in every experience life brings us. There is no escaping it. Again it is said in the teachings: "Better not to begin. Once you begin, better to finish it." So you had better not step onto the spiritual path unless you must. Once you have stepped foot on the path, you have really done it, you cannot step back. There is no way of escaping.

Q: Having stumbled around various spiritual centers, I feel that a personality like Marpa must be a very troublesome phenomenon for most addicts along these lines. For here is a man who seems not to be doing any of the things that everybody says will get you there. He's not ascetic, he doesn't abnegate. He looks after his everyday affairs. He is a normal human being and yet, apparently, he is a teacher of enormous capability. Is Marpa the only one who has made the most of the possibilities for a normal man without going through all the tremendous pain of asceticism and the discipline of purification?

A: Of course Marpa is an example of the possibilities open to us. However, he did experience tremendous discipline and training while he was in India. By studying strenuously under Indian teachers he prepared his path. But I think we must understand the true meaning of the words "discipline" and "asceticism." The basic idea of asceticism, leading a life according to the dharma, is to be fundamentally sane. If you find that leading an ordinary life is a sane thing to do, that is dharma. At the same time you could find that leading the life of an ascetic yogi, as described in the texts, could become an expression of insanity. It depends upon the individual. It is a question of what is sane for you, the really solid, sound, stable approach to life. The Buddha, for example, was not a religious fanatic, attempting to act in accordance with some high ideal. He just dealt with people simply, openly and very wisely. His wisdom came from transcendental common sense. His teaching was sound and open.

The problem seems to be that people worry about a conflict between the religious and the profane. They find it very difficult to reconcile so called "higher consciousness" with practical affairs. But the categories of higher and lower, religious and profane, do not really seem relevant to a basically sane approach to life.

Marpa was just an ordinary person, involved in living every detail of his life. He never tried to be someone special. When he lost his temper, he just lost it and beat people. He just did it. He never acted or pretended. Religious fanatics, on the other hand, are always trying to live up to some model of how it all is supposed to be. They try to win people over by coming on very strong and frantic, as though they were completely pure and good. But I think that attempting to prove that you are good indicates fear of some kind. Marpa, however, had nothing to prove. He was just a very sane and ordinary solid citizen, and a very enlightened person at the same time. In fact, he is the father of the whole Kagyü lineage. All the teachings we are studying and practicing spring from him.

Q: There is a Zen expression: "At first the mountains are mountains and streams are streams. Then the mountains are not mountains and streams are not streams. But in the end, mountains are mountains again and streams are streams again." Well, aren't we all in the stage where mountains are not mountains and streams are not streams? Yet you are emphasizing this ordinary quality. Don't we have to go through this "not ordinary" period before we can really be ordinary?

A: Marpa was very upset when his son was killed, and one of his disciples said, "You used to tell us that everything is illusion. How about the death of your son? Isn't it illusion?" And Marpa replied, "True, but my son's death is a super-illusion."

When we first experience true ordinariness, it is something very extraordinarily ordinary, so much so that we would say that mountains are not mountains any more or streams streams any more, because we see them as so ordinary, so precise, so "as they are." This extraordinariness derives from the experience of discovery. But eventually this super-ordinariness, this precision, becomes an everyday event, something we live with all the time, truly ordinary, and we are back where we started: the mountains are mountains and streams are streams. Then we can relax.

Q: How do you take off your suit of armor? How do you open yourself?

A: It is not a question of *how* you do it. There is no ritual or ceremony or formula for opening. The first obstacle is the question itself: "How?" If you don't question yourself, don't watch yourself, then you just do it. We do not consider how we are going to vomit; we just vomit. There is no time to think about it; it just happens. If we are very tense, then we will have tremendous pain and will not really be able to vomit properly. We will try to swallow it back, try to struggle with our illness. We have to learn to relax when we are sick.

Q: When the situations of life start to become your guru, does it matter what form the situation takes? Does it matter what situation you find yourself in?

A: You have no choice at all. Whatever happens is an expression of the guru. The situation could be painful or inspiring, but both pain and pleasure are one in this openness of seeing the situation as guru.

Initiation

Most of the people who have come to study with me have done so because they have heard of me personally, of my reputation as a meditation teacher and Tibetan lama. But how many people would have come had we first bumped into each other on the road or met in a restaurant? Very few people would be inspired to study Buddhism and meditation by such a meeting. Rather people seem to be inspired by the fact that I am a meditation teacher from exotic Tibet, the eleventh reincarnation of the Trungpa Tulku.

So people come and seek initiation from me, initiation into the Buddhist teachings and the sangha, the community of meditators on the path. But what does this initiation really mean? There is a long and great tradition of handing down the wisdom of the Buddhist lineage from one generation of meditators to the next, and this transmission is connected with initiation. But what is it all about?

It really seems worthwhile to be cynical in this regard. People would like to receive initiation: they would like to join the club, receive a title, obtain wisdom. Personally, I do not wish to play on people's weakness, their desire to get something extraordinary. Some people will buy a painting by Picasso simply because of the artist's name. They will pay thousands of dollars without considering whether what they are buying is worthwhile as art. They are buying the painting's credentials, the name, accepting reputation and rumor as their guarantee of artistic merit. There is no hard intelligence in such an act.

Or someone might join a club, be initiated into a particular organization because he feels starved, worthless. The group is fat and wealthy and he wants someone to feed him. He gets fed and becomes fat as he expected, but then what? Who is deceiving whom? Is the teacher or guru deceiving himself, expanding his ego? "I have such a large flock of followers who have been initiated." Or is he deceiving his students, leading them to believe that they have become wiser, more spiritual, simply because they have committed themselves to his organization and have been labeled monks, yogis, whatever titles they may have received? There are so many different titles to receive. Do these names, credentials bring us any real benefit? Do they really? Half an hour's ceremony does not bring us to the next stage of enlightenment; let's face facts. I personally have tremendous devotion to and faith in the Buddhist lineage and the power of the teachings, but not in a simple-minded way.

We must approach spirituality with a hard kind of intelligence. If we go to hear a teacher speak, we should not allow ourselves to be carried away by his reputation and charisma, but we should properly experience each word of his lecture or each aspect of the meditation technique being taught. We must make a clear and intelligent relationship with the teachings and the man teaching. Such intelligence has nothing to do with emotionalism or romanticizing the guru. It has nothing to do with gullibly accepting impressive credentials, nor is it a matter of joining a club that we might be enriched.

It is not a matter of finding a wise guru from whom we can buy or steal wisdom. True initiation involves dealing honestly and straight forwardly with our spiritual friend and ourselves. So we have to make some effort to expose ourselves and our self-deceptions. We have to surrender and expose the raw and rugged quality of our ego.

The Sanskrit equivalent for "initiation" is *abhisheka* which means "sprinkle," "pour," "annointment." And if there is pouring, there must be a vessel into which the pouring can fall. If we really commit ourselves by opening to our spiritual friend properly, completely, becoming a vessel into which his communication may fall, then he will also open and initiation will occur. This is the meaning of abhisheka or "the meeting of the two minds" of teacher and student.

Such opening does not involve ingratiation, trying to please or impress our spiritual friend. The situation is similar to that in which a doctor, realizing that there is something wrong with you, takes you from your home, by force if necessary, and operates on your body without an anaesthetic. You might find this kind of treatment a bit too violent and painful, but then you begin to realize how much real communication—being in touch with life—costs.

Monetary donations to a spiritual cause, contributions of physical labor, involvement with a particular guru, none of these necessarily mean that we have actually committed ourselves to openness. More likely these kinds of commitment are simply ways of proving that we have joined the side of "right." The guru seems to be a wise person. He knows what he is doing and we would like to be on his side, the safe side, the good side, in order to secure our well-being and success. But once we have attached ourselves to his side, the side of sanity, the side of stability, the side of wisdom, then to our surprise we discover that we have not succeeded in securing ourselves at all, because we have only committed our facade, our face, our suit of armor. We have not totally committed *ourselves.*

Then we are forced to open from behind. To our horror we find that there is no place to run. We are discovered in the act of hiding behind a facade, exposed on all sides; the padding and armor that we have worn are all stripped away. There is no longer any place to hide. Shocking! Everything is revealed, our petty pretense and egotism. At this point we might realize that our clumsy attempt to wear a mask has all along been pointless.

Still we attempt to rationalize this painful situation, trying to find some way to protect ourselves, some way to explain our predicament to ego's satisfaction. We look at it this way and that way, and our mind is extremely busy. Ego is very professional, overwhelmingly efficient in its way. When we think that we are working on the forward-moving process of attempting to empty ourselves out, we find ourselves going backwards, trying to secure ourselves, filling ourselves up. And this confusion continues and intensifies until we finally discover that we are totally lost, that we have lost our ground, that there is no starting point or middle or end because our mind has been so overwhelmed by our own defense mechanisms. So the only alternative seems to be to just give in and let be. Our clever ideas and smart solutions do us no good, because we have been overwhelmed with too many ideas; we do not know which ideas to choose, which ideas will provide us with the best way to work on ourselves. Our mind is overcrowded with extraordinary, intelligent, logical, scientific and cunning suggestions. But somehow there are too many and we do not know which suggestion to take.

So at last we might really give up all these complications and just allow some space, just give in. This is the moment when abhisheka—sprinkling and pouring—really takes place, because we are open and are really giving up the whole attempt to do anything, giving up all the busyness and overcrowding. Finally we have been forced to really stop properly, which is quite a rare occurrence for us.

We have so many different defense mechanisms fashioned out of the knowledge we have received, the reading we have done, the experiences we have undergone, the dreams we have dreamed. But finally we begin to question what spirituality means really. Is it simply a matter of attempting to be religious, pious and good? Or is it trying to know more than other people, trying to learn more about the significance of life? What does it really mean, spirituality? The familiar theories of our family church and its doctrine are always available, but somehow these are not the answers we seek; they are a bit too ineffective, not applicable. So we fall away from the doctrines and dogmas of the religion we were born to.

We might decide that spirituality is something very exciting and colorful. It is a matter of exploring ourselves in the tradition of some exotic and different sect or religion. We adopt another kind of spirituality, behaving in a certain way, attempting to change our tone of voice and eating habits and our behavior in general. But after a while such self-conscious attempts to be spiritual begin to feel too clumsy and obvious, too familiar. We intend these patterns of behavior to become habitual, second nature, but somehow they do not completely become a part of us. Much as we would like these "enlightened" behavior patterns to become a natural part of our makeup, neurosis is still present in our minds. We begin to wonder: "If I have been acting in accordance with the sacred scriptures of the such and such tradition, how could this happen? This must be due to my confusion, of course. But what do I do next?" Confusion still continues in spite of our faithful adherence to the scriptures. Neuroticism and discontent go on. Nothing really clicks; we have not connected with the teachings.

At this point we really need "the meeting of the two minds." Without abhisheka our attempts to achieve spirituality will result in no more than a huge spiritual collection rather than real surrender. We have been collecting different behavior patterns, different manners of speech, dress, thought, whole different ways of acting. And all of it is merely a collection we are attempting to impose upon ourselves.

Abhisheka, true initiation, is born out of surrender. We open ourselves to the situation as it is, and then we make real communication with the teacher. In any event, the guru is already there with us in a state of openness; and if we open ourselves, are willing to give up our collections, then initiation takes place. There is no "sacred" ceremony necessary. In fact, considering initiation "sacred" is probably seduction by what Buddhists refer to as "the daughters of Mara." Mara represents the neurotic tendency of mind, the unbalanced state of being, and he sends his daughters to seduce us. When the daughters of Mara take part in initiation in which the meeting of the two minds is actually taking place, they will say, "You feel peaceful? That is because you are receiving spiritual instruction, because this is a spiritual thing that is happening to you, it is sacred." They have very sweet voices and bring a lovely, beautiful message, and they seduce us into thinking that this communication, this "meeting of the two minds" is a "big deal." Then we begin to give birth to further samsaric patterns of mind. It is similar to the Christian idea of biting the apple; it is temptation. When we regard abhisheka

as sacred, then the precision and sharpness immediately begin
to fall away because we have begun to evaluate. We hear the
voices of the daughters of Mara congratulating us that we have
managed to do such a holy thing. They are dancing around us
and playing music in the pretense of honoring us on this cere-
monial occasion.

The meeting of the two minds really takes place very naturally. Both the instructor and the student meet in a state of
openness in which they both realize that openness is the most
insignificant thing in the whole world. It is completely insignificant, truly ordinary, absolutely nothing. When we are able
to see ourselves and the world in this way, then transmission
is directly taking place. In the Tibetan tradition this way of
seeing things is called "ordinary mind," *thamal-gyi-shépa.*
It is the most insignificant thing of all, complete openness, the
absence of any kind of collection or evaluation. We could say
that such insignificance is very significant, that such ordinariness is truly extraordinary. But this would just be further
seduction by the daughters of Mara. Eventually we must give
up trying to be something special.

Q: It seems that I cannot get away from trying to secure myself. What should I do?
A: You want so much to be secure that the idea of trying *not*
to secure yourself has become a game, a big joke, and a way
of securing yourself. You are so concerned about watching
yourself and watching yourself watching, and watching yourself watching yourself watching. It goes on and on and on. It is
quite a common phenomenon.

What is really needed is for you to stop caring altogether, to
completely drop the whole concern. The overlapping complications, building an extremely fine lie detector and a detector

for the lie detector as well, such complicated structures have to be cleared away. You try to secure yourself and, having achieved security, then you also attempt to secure that as well. Such fortifications could extend to an infinite empire. You might just own a tiny little castle, but the scope of your protection could extend to cover the entire earth. If you really want to secure yourself completely, there is literally no limit to the efforts you can make.

So it is necessary to drop altogether the idea of security and see the irony of your attempts to secure yourself, the irony of your overlapping structure of self-protection. You have to give up the watcher of the watcher of the watcher. In order to do this, one has to drop the first watcher, the intention of protection itself.

Q: I don't know what nationality to bring up, but if we were Indians, for instance, you wouldn't speak to us this way, would you? I mean, it's because we are Americans and are so much into *doing* things that you have to speak to us this way. If we were given to doing nothing, just sitting around, you wouldn't speak to us like this.

A: That is a very interesting point. I think the style in which the teachings are presented depends upon how much the audience is involved with the speed of materialism. America has achieved an extremely sophisticated level of physical materialism. However, the potential for being involved in this kind of speed is not limited to Americans, it is universal, world-wide. If India reaches the stages of economic development that America has attained, where people have achieved and have become disillusioned with physical materialism, then they will be coming to listen to such a lecture. But at this time I do not think there would be an audience for this kind of lecture anywhere other than in the West, because people elsewhere are not yet tired enough of the speed of physical materialism. They are still saving money to buy bicycles on the way to automobiles.

Self-Deception

Self-deception is a constant problem as we progress along a spiritual path. Ego is always trying to achieve spirituality. It is rather like wanting to witness your own funeral. For instance, in the beginning we might approach our spiritual friend hoping to get something wonderful from him. This approach is called "hunting the guru." Traditionally, it is compared to hunting the musk deer. The hunter stalks the deer, kills it, and removes the musk. We could take this approach to the guru and spirituality, but it would be self-deception. It would have nothing to do with real opening or surrender.

Or we might falsely assume that initiation means transplantation, transplanting the spiritual power of the teachings from the guru's heart into our own. This mentality regards the teachings as something foreign to us. It is similar to the idea of transplanting a real heart or, for that matter, a head. A foreign element is transplanted into us from outside our body. We might tend to appraise our potential transplant. Perhaps our old head is not suitable, perhaps it should be thrown into the rubbish heap. We deserve a better head, a fresh one, a more intelligent one with lots of brains. We are so concerned with what we are going to get out of our potential operation that we have forgotten the doctor who is going to perform it.

Have we stopped to make a relationship with our physician? Is he competent? Is the head we have chosen really suitable? Might not our doctor have something to say about our choice of heads? Perhaps our body would reject that head. We are so concerned with what we think we are going to *get*, that we ignore what is really happening, our relationship with our doctor, our illness, what this new head really is.

This approach to the process of initiation is very romantic and not at all valid. So we need someone personally concerned with us as we really are, we need a person to play the part of mirror. Whenever we are involved with any kind of self-deception, it is necessary that the whole process be revealed, opened. Any grasping attitude must be exposed.

Real initiation takes place in terms of "the meeting of the two minds." It is a matter of being what you really are and of relating to the spiritual friend as he or she is. This is the true situation in which initiation might occur, because the idea of having an operation and fundamentally changing yourself is completely unrealistic. No one can really change your personality absolutely. No one can turn you completely upside down and inside out. The existing material, that which is already there, must be used. You must accept yourself as you are, instead of as you would like to be, which means giving up self-deception and wishful thinking. Your whole make-up and personality characteristics must be recognized, accepted, and then you might find some inspiration.

At this point, if you express a willingness to work with your physician by committing yourself into the hospital, then the doctor for his part will make available a room and whatever else is needed. So both sides would be creating a situation of open communication, which is the fundamental meaning of "the meeting of the two minds." This is the real way of uniting the blessing or *adhishthana*, the spiritual essence of the guru, and your own spiritual essence. The external teacher, the guru, opens himself and, because you also are open, because you are "awake," there is the meeting of two elements which are identical. This is the true meaning of abhisheka, initiation. It is not a matter of joining a club, of becoming one of the flock, a sheep with your owner's initials branded on your behind.

So now we can examine what comes after abhisheka. Having experienced the meeting of the two minds, we have established real communication with our spiritual friend. We have not only opened ourselves, but we have also experienced a flash of insight, an instant understanding of part of the teachings. The teacher created the situation, we experienced this flash, and everything seems to be fine.

At first we are very excited, everything is beautiful. We might find that for several days we feel very "high" and excited. It seems we have already achieved the level of Buddhahood. No mundane concerns bother us at all, everything goes very smoothly, instantaneous meditation occurs all the time. It is a continuous experience of our moment of openness with the guru. This is quite common. At this point many people might feel that they do not need to work further with their spiritual friend, and possibly they might leave, go away. I heard many stories of this happening in the East: certain students met their teacher and received an instant enlightenment experience and then left. They tried to preserve that experience, but as time went on it became just a memory, words and ideas which they repeated to themselves.

Quite possibly your first reaction after such an experience would be to write it down in your diary, explaining in words everything that happened. You would attempt to anchor yourself to the experience through your writings and memoirs, by discussing it with people, or by talking to people who witnessed you having the experience.

Or a person might have gone to the East and had this sort of experience and then come back to the West. His friends might find him tremendously changed. He might look calmer, quieter, wiser. Many people might ask him for help and advice with their personal problems, might ask for his opinion of their experience of spirituality. In the beginning, his way of helping other people would be genuine, relating their problems to his own experience in the East, telling people beautiful and genuine stories of what happened to him. It would be very inspiring for him.

But at some stage in this sort of situation something tends to go wrong. The memory of that sudden flash of insight that a person has experienced loses its intensity. It does not last because he regards it as being external to himself. He feels that he has had a sudden experience of the awakened state of mind and that it belongs to the category of holiness, spiritual experience. He valued the experience highly and then communicated it to the ordinary and familiar world of his homeland, to his enemies and friends, parents and relatives, to all those people and attachments which he now feels he has transcended and overcome. But now the experience is no longer with him. There is just the memory. And yet, having proclaimed his experience and knowledge to other people, he obviously cannot go back and say what he said previously was false. He could not do that at all; it would be too humiliating. Moreover, he still has faith in the experience, that something profound really happened. But unfortunately the experience is no longer present at this very moment, because he used and evaluated it.

Speaking generally what happens is that, once we have actually opened, "flashed," in the second moment we realize that we are open and the idea of evaluation suddenly appears. "Wow, fantastic, I have to catch that, I have to capture and keep it because it is a very rare and valuable experience." So we try to hold onto the experience and the problems start there, from regarding the real experience of openness as something valuable. As soon as we try to capture the experience, a whole series of chain reactions sets in.

If we regard something as valuable and extraordinary, then it becomes quite separate from us. For instance, we do not regard our eyes, body, hands or head as valuable, because we know they are a part of us. Of course, if we lost them, any of them, our automatic reaction would be that we had lost such a valuable thing—"I have lost my head, I have lost my arm, it is impossible to replace!" Then we realize that it is a valuable thing. When something is removed from us, we have the opportunity to realize that it is valuable. But when we have it with us all the time, when it is part of our entire make-up, then we cannot value it particularly; it is just there. The evaluation comes from the fear of being separated, which is just what keeps us separated. We consider any sudden inspiration to be extraordinarily important, because we are afraid of losing it. That very point, that very moment, is when self-deception comes in. In other words, we lost faith in the experience of openness and its relationship to us.

Somehow we lost the unity of openness and what we are. Openness became a separate thing, and then we began to play games. It is obvious that we cannot say that we have lost the openness. "I used to have it, but I have lost it." We cannot say that, because that will destroy our status as an accomplished person. So the part of self-deception is to retell the stories. We would rather tell stories than actually experience openness, because stories are very vivid and enjoyable. "When I was with my guru, such and such happened; he said such and such things and opened me in such and such a way, etc., etc." So self-deception, in this case, means trying to recreate a past experience again and again, instead of actually having the experience in the present moment. In order to have the experience now, one would have to give up the evaluation of how wonderful the flash was, because it is this memory which keeps it distant. If we had the experience continuously it would seem quite ordinary, and it is this ordinariness that we cannot accept. "If only I could have that wonderful experience of openness again!" So we keep ourselves busy not having it, remembering it. This is self-deception's game.

Self-deception needs the idea of evaluation and a very long memory. Thinking back, we feel nostalgic, getting a kick from our memories, but we do not know where we are at this very moment. We remember the "good times," the "good old days." We do not allow our depression to emerge at all, we do not want to accept the suspicion that we are out of touch with something. Whenever the possibility of depression arises and the feeling of loss is about to occur, the defensive nature of ego immediately brings to mind memories and words we have heard in the past in order to comfort us. Thus ego is continually looking for inspiration which has no root in the present; it is a continual running back. This is the more complicated action of self-deception: one does not allow depression to come into being at all. "Since I have received such great blessings and been fortunate enough to have these wonderful spiritual experiences, how can I possibly say that I am depressed? Impossible, there is no room for depression."

There is the story of the great Tibetan teacher, Marpa. When Marpa first met his own teacher, Naropa, Naropa created an altar which he said was the embodiment of the wisdom of a particular *heruka*. Both the shrine and Naropa contained tremendous spiritual energy and power, and Naropa asked Marpa to which one he would prostrate in order to experience the sudden realization of enlightenment. Marpa, being a scholar, considered that the guru lives in the flesh, an ordinary human body, while his creation, the altar, is a pure body of wisdom, having nothing to do with human imperfection. So Marpa prostrated to the shrine. And then Naropa said, "I am afraid your inspiration is going to fade. You have made the wrong choice. This shrine is my creation, and without me the shrine would not be here at all. The issue of human body versus wisdom body is irrelevant. The great display of the mandala was merely my creation."

This story illustrates the principle of dream, hope, wish, as self-deception. As long as you regard yourself or any part of your experience as the "dream come true," then you are involved in self-deception. Self-deception seems always to depend upon the dream world, because you would like to see what you have not yet seen, rather that what you are now seeing. You will not accept that whatever is here now *is* what is, nor are you willing to go on with the situation as it is. Thus, self-deception always manifests itself in terms of trying to create or recreate a dream world, the nostalgia of the dream experience. And the opposite of self-deception is just working with the facts of life.

If one searches for any kind of bliss or joy, the realization of one's imagination and dream, then, equally, one is going to suffer failure and depression. This is the whole point: a fear of separation, the hope of attaining union, these are not just manifestations of or the actions of ego or self-deception, as if ego were somehow a real thing which performed certain actions. Ego *is* the actions, the mental events. Ego *is* the fear of losing openness, the fear of losing the egoless state. This is the meaning of self-deception, in this case—ego crying that it has lost the egoless state, its dream of attainment. Fear, hope, loss, gain—these are the on-going action of the dream of ego, the self-perpetuating, self-maintaining structure which is self-deception.

So the real experience, beyond the dream world, is the beauty and color and excitement of the real experience of *now* in everyday life. When we face things as they are, we give up the hope of something better. There will be no magic, because we cannot tell ourselves to get out of our depression. Depression and ignorance, the emotions, whatever we experience, are all real and contain tremendous truth. If we really want to learn and see the experience of truth, we have to be where we are. The whole thing is just a matter of being a grain of sand.

Q: Would you talk some more about the mechanics of this force of despair? I can understand why despair might occur, but why does bliss occur?

A: It is possible in the beginning to force oneself into the experience of bliss. It is a kind of self-hypnosis, in that we refuse to see the background of what we are. We focus only upon the immediate experience of bliss. We ignore the entire basic ground, where we really are at, so to speak, and we work ourselves up to an experience of tremendous joy. The trouble is, this kind of experience is based purely upon watching oneself. It is a completely dualistic approach. We would like to experience something, and by working very hard we do actually achieve it. However, once we come down from our "high," once we realize that we are still here, like a black rock standing in the middle of an ocean of waves, then depression sets in. We would like to get drunk, intoxicated, absorbed into the entire universe, but somehow it does not happen. We are still here, which is always the first thing to bring us down. Later all the other games of self-deception, of trying to feed oneself further, begin because one is trying to protect oneself completely. It is the "watcher" principle.

Q: You speak of people experiencing something and then grasping it intellectually, labeling it saying, "That's fantastic." This seems to be an almost automatic reaction. Could you go through the ways in which people begin to get away from doing this? It seems to me that the more you try to stop evaluating, the more you are evaluating.

A: Well, once you realize that you are actually doing this and are not getting anything from it, then I think you begin to find your way out. One begins to see that the whole process is part of a huge game which is not really profitable, because you are continuously building rather than coming to an understanding of anything. There is no magic or trick involved. The only thing to do is to quite painfully unmask.

Perhaps you will have to build and build until you realize the futility of attempting to achieve spirituality. Your entire mind might become completely overcrowded with your struggle. In fact, you might not know whether you are coming or going, to the point where you become completely exhausted. Then you might learn a very useful lesson: to give up the whole thing, to be nothing. You might even experience a

yearning to be nothing. There seem to be two solutions: either
to simply unmask, or else to build and build, strive and strive,
until you reach a crescendo and then drop the whole thing.

Q: What happens when one says, "Wow, I've made it." That
doesn't blow the whole trip, does it?
A: Not necessarily. But then, what happens next? Do you
want to repeat your experience again and again, rather than
working with the present situation of what is? One could experience tremendous joy in the first flash of openness, which is
quite beautiful. But what comes afterwards is important:
whether one is working to grasp and recreate that experience
or whether one is letting be, allowing that experience to be
just one experience, not attempting to recreate the first flash.

Q: You are ambitious, building all the time, and the more
you think about it, the worse it gets. So you try to just run away
from the whole thing, try not to think about it, try to lose yourself in all sorts of escapes. What does this mean and how can
one get over the fact that, the more one thinks about enlightenment and tries to find out about it, the worse things become and
the more conceptualizations accumulate? What do you do?
A: That is very obvious. You drop searching for anything
altogether, drop trying to discover anything, trying to prove
yourself.

Q: But sometimes one might have an active feeling of running away, and that is not the same thing as not doing anything
at all.
A: Once you try to run away, you find that not only are you
being chased from behind, but there are also people coming
towards you from the front as well. Eventually there is no

room to run. You are completely trapped. Then the only thing
to do is really, simply to give in.

Q: What does that mean?
A: Well, one has to experience it. It means to stop trying to
go anywhere, both in terms of getting away from and of running to, because both are the same thing.

Q: Is self-remembering or observing oneself incongruent
with giving in and being here?
A: Self-remembering is quite a dangerous technique, actually. It could involve watching yourself and your actions
like a hungry cat watching mice, or else it could be an intelligent gesture of being where you are. The whole point is that,
if you have any idea of relationship—I am experiencing this,
I am doing this—then "I" and "this" are very strong person-
alities, equally. Somehow there will be a conflict between "I"
and "this." It is rather like saying that "this" is the mother
and "I" the father. With two such polar extremes involved
you are bound to give birth to something. So the whole idea is
to let "this" not be there, and then "I" will not be there. Or
else, "I" is not there, therefore "this" is not there. It is not a
matter of telling it to yourself, but of feeling it, a real experience. You must take away the watcher, the observer of the two
extremes. Once the watcher is removed, then the whole structure falls apart. The dichotomy remains in existence only so
long as there is an observer to keep the whole picture together.
You must remove the watcher and the very complicated bureaucracy he creates to insure that nothing is missed by central headquarters. Once we take away the watcher, there is a
tremendous amount of space, because he and his bureaucracy
take up so much room. If we eliminate the filter of "I" and

"other," then the space becomes sharp and precise and intelligent. Space contains the tremendous precision of being able to work with the situations in it. One does not really need the "watcher" or "observer" at all.

Q: Does the watcher exist because you want to be living at what seems a higher level, whereas if you just let go, perhaps you would be *here*?

A: Yes, that is true. When the watcher disappears, the notion of higher and lower levels does not apply, so there is no longer any inclination to struggle, attempting to get higher. Then you just are where you are.

Q: Can you remove the watcher by force? Wouldn't that be the game of evaluation again?

A: You do not have to regard the watcher as a villain. Once you begin to understand that the purpose of meditation is not to get higher but to be present, here, then the watcher is not efficient enough to perform that function, and it automatically falls away. The basic quality of the watcher is to try to be extremely efficient and active. But total awareness is something you already have, so ambitious or so called "efficient" attempts to be aware are self-defeating. As the watcher begins to realize that it is irrelevant, it falls away.

Q: Can there be awareness without a watcher?

A: Yes, because the watcher is only paranoia. You could have complete openness, a panoramic situation, without having to discriminate between two parties, "I" and "other."

Q: Would that awareness involve feelings of bliss?

A: I do not think so, because bliss is a very individual experience. You are separate and you are experiencing your bliss. When the watcher is gone, there is no evaluation of the experience as being pleasant or painful. When you have panoramic awareness without the evaluation of the watcher, then the bliss becomes irrelevant, by the very fact that there is no one experiencing it.

The Hard Way

Inasmuch as no one is going to save us, to the extent that no one is going magically to enlighten us, the path we are discussing is called the "hard way." This path does not conform to our expectation that involvement with the Buddhist teaching will be gentle, peaceful, pleasant, compassionate. It is the hard way, a simple meeting of two minds: if you open your mind, if you are willing to meet, then the teacher opens his mind as well. It is not a question of magic; the condition of openness is a mutual creation.

Generally, when we speak of freedom or liberation or spiritual understanding, we think that to attain these things we need do nothing at all, that someone else will take care of us. "You are all right, don't worry, don't cry, you're going to be all right. I'll take care of you." We tend to think that all we have to do is make a commitment to the organization, pay our initiation fee, sign the register and then follow the instructions given us. "I am firmly convinced that your organization is valid, it answers all my questions. You may program me in any way. If you want to put me into difficult situations, do so. I leave everything to you." This attitude supplies the comfort of having to do nothing but follow orders. Everything is left to the other person, to instruct you and relieve you of your shortcomings. But to our surprise things do not work that way. The idea that we do not have to do anything on our own is extremely wishful thinking.

It takes tremendous effort to work one's way through the difficulties of the path and actually get into the situations of life thoroughly and properly. So the whole point of the hard way seems to be that some individual effort must be made by the student to acknowledge himself, to go through the process of unmasking. One must be willing to stand alone, which is difficult.

This is not to say that the point of the hard way is that we must be heroic. The attitude of "heroism" is based upon the assumption that we are bad, impure, that we are not worthy, are not ready for spiritual understanding. We must reform ourselves, be different from what we are. For instance, if we are middle class Americans, we must give up our jobs or drop out of college, move out of our suburban homes, let our hair grow, perhaps try drugs. If we are hippies, we must give up drugs, cut our hair short, throw away our torn jeans. We think that we are special, heroic, that we are turning away from temptation. We become vegetarians and we become this and that. There are so many things to become. We think our path is spiritual because it is literally against the flow of what we used to be, but it is merely the way of false heroism, and the only one who is heroic in this way is ego.

We can carry this sort of false heroism to great extremes, getting ourselves into completely austere situations. If the teaching with which we are engaged recommends standing on our heads for twenty-four hours a day, we do it. We purify ourselves, perform austerities, and we feel extremely cleansed, reformed, virtuous. Perhaps there seems to be nothing wrong with it at the time.

We might attempt to imitate certain spiritual paths, such as the American Indian path or the Hindu path or the Japanese Zen Buddhist path. We might abandon our suits and collars and ties, our belts and trousers and shoes in an attempt to follow their example. Or we may decide to go to northern India in order to join the Tibetans. We might wear Tibetan clothing and adopt Tibetan customs. This will seem to be the "hard way," because there will always be obstacles and temptations to distract us from our purpose.

Sitting in a Hindu ashram, we have not eaten chocolate for six or seven months, so we dream of chocolate, or other dishes that we like. Perhaps we are nostalgic on Christmas or New Year's Day. But still we think we have found the path of discipline. We have struggled through the difficulties of this path and have become quite competent, masters of discipline of some sort. We expect the magic and wisdom of our training and practice to bring us into the right state of mind. Sometimes we think we have achieved our goal. Perhaps we are completely "high" or absorbed for a period of six or seven months. Later our ecstasy disappears. And so it goes, on and on, on and off. How are we going to deal with this situation? We may be able to stay "high" or blissful for a very long time, but then we have to come back or come down or return to normal.

I am not saying that foreign or disciplinary traditions are not applicable to the spiritual path. Rather, I am saying that we have the notion that there must be some kind of medicine or magic potion to help us attain the right state of mind. This seems to be coming at the problem backwards. We hope that by manipulating matter, the physical world, we can achieve wisdom and understanding. We may even expect expert scientists to do it for us. They might put us into a hospital, administer the correct drugs and lift us into a high state of consciousness. But I think, unfortunately, that this is impossible, we cannot escape what we are, we carry it with us all the time.

So the point we come back to is that some kind of *real* gift or sacrifice is needed if we are to open ourselves completely. This gift may take any form. But in order for it to be meaningful, it must entail giving up our hope of getting something in return. It does not matter how many titles we have, nor how many suits of exotic clothes we have worn through, nor how many philosophies, commitments and sacramental ceremonies we have participated in. We must give up our ambition to get something in return for our gift. That is the really hard way.

We may have had a wonderful time touring around Japan. We may have enjoyed Japanese culture, beautiful Zen temples, magnificent works of art. And not only did we find these experiences beautiful, but they said something to us as well. This culture is the creation of a whole lifestyle completely different from that of the Western world, and these creations spoke to us. But to what extent does the exquisiteness of culture and images, the beauty of the external forms really shake us, deal with us? We do not know. We merely want to savor our beautiful memories. We do not want to question our experiences too closely. It is a sensitive area.

Or perhaps a certain guru has initiated us in a very moving, extremely meaningful ceremony. That ceremony was real and direct and beautiful, but how much of the experience are we willing to question? It is private, too sensitive to question. We would rather hoard and preserve the flavor and beauty of the experience so that, when bad times come, when we are depressed and down, we can bring that memory to mind in order to comfort ourselves, to tell ourselves that we have actually done something worthwhile, that, yes, we are on the path. This does not seem to be the hard way at all.

On the contrary, it would seem that we have been collecting rather than giving. If we reconsider our spiritual shopping, can we remember an occasion when we gave something completely and properly, opened ourselves and gave everything? Have we ever unmasked, stripping out of our suit of armor and our shirt and skin and flesh and veins, right down to the heart? Have we really experienced the process of stripping and opening and giving? That is the fundamental question. We must really surrender, give something, give something up in a very painful way. We must begin to dismantle the basic structure of this ego we have managed to create. The process of dismantling, undoing, opening, giving up, is the real learning process. How much of this ingrown toenail situation have we decided to give up? Most likely, we have not managed to give up anything at all. We have only collected, built, adding layer upon layer. So the prospect of the hard way is very threatening.

The problem is that we tend to seek an easy and painless answer. But this kind of solution does not apply to the spiritual path, which many of us should not have begun at all. Once we commit ourselves to the spiritual path, it is very painful and we are in for it. We have committed ourselves to the pain of exposing ourselves, of taking off our clothes, our skin, nerves, heart, brains, until we are exposed to the universe. Nothing will be left. It will be terrible, excruciating, but that is the way it is.

Somehow we find ourselves in the company of a strange doctor. He is going to operate on us, but he is not going to use an anaesthetic because he really wants to communicate with our illness. He is not going to allow us to put on our facade of spirituality, psychological sophistication, false psychological illness or any other disguise. We wish we had never met him. We wish we understood how to anaesthetize ourselves. But now we are in for it. There is no way out. Not because he is so powerful. We could tell him goodbye in a minute and leave. But we have exposed so much to this physician and, if we have to do it all over again, it will be very painful. We do not want to have to do it again. So now we have to go all the way.

Being with this doctor is extremely uncomfortable for us because we are continually trying to con him, although we know that he sees through our games. This operation is his only way to communicate with us, so we must accept it; we must open ourselves to the hard way, to this operation. The more we ask questions—"What are you going to do to me?"— the more embarrassed we become, because we know what we are. It is an extremely narrow path with no escape, a painful path. We must surrender ourselves completely and communicate with this physician. Moreover, we must unmask our expectations of magic on the part of the guru, that with his magical powers he can initiate us in certain extraordinary and painless ways. We have to give up looking for a painless operation, give up hope that he will use an anaesthetic or sedative so that when we wake up everything will be perfect. We must be willing to communicate in a completely open and direct way with our spiritual friend and with our life, without any hidden corners. It is difficult and painful, the hard way.

Q.   Is exposing yourself something that just happens, or is there a way of doing it, a way of opening?
A: I think that if you are already committed to the process of exposing yourself, then the less you try to open the more

the process of opening becomes obvious. I would say it is an automatic action rather than something that you have to do. At the beginning when we discussed surrendering, I said that once you have exposed everything to your spiritual friend, then you do not have to do anything at all. It is a matter of just accepting what is, which we tend to do in any case. We often find ourselves in situations completely naked, wishing we had clothes to cover ourselves. These embarrassing situations always come to us in life.

Q: Must we have a spiritual friend before we can expose ourselves, or can we just open ourselves to the situations of life?
A: I think you need someone to watch you do it, because then it will seem more real to you. It is easy to undress in a room with no one else around, but we find it difficult to undress ourselves in a room full of people.

Q: So it is really exposing ourselves to ourselves?
A: Yes. But we do not see it that way. We have a strong consciousness of the audience because we have so much awareness of ourselves.

Q: I do not see why performing austerities and mastering discipline is not the "real" hard way.
A: You can deceive yourself, thinking you are going through the hard way, when actually you are not. It is like being in an heroic play. The "soft way" is very much involved with the experience of heroism, while the hard way is much more personal. Having gone through the way of heroism, you still have the hard way to go through, which is a very shocking thing to discover.

Q: Is it necessary to go through the heroic way first and is it necessary to persevere in the heroic way in order to continue on the truly hard way?

A: I don't think so. This is what I am trying to point out. If you involve yourself with the heroic way, you add layers or skins to your personality because you think you have achieved something. Later, to your surprise, you discover that something else is needed. One must *remove* the layers, the skins.

Q: You speak of the necessity to experience excruciating pain. Can an understanding of the unmasking process make it unnecessary to go through the pain?

A: That is a very tricky proposition. Understanding does not mean that you actually do it; you just understand it. We can understand the physiological process of how someone is tortured and how they experience pain, but the actual experience would be altogether different. The philosophical or intellectual understanding of pain is not enough. You must actually feel something properly. The only way to get to the heart of the matter is to actually experience it for yourself, but you do not have to create painful situations. These situations will occur with the help of a spiritual friend who is a doctor with a sharp knife.

Q: If you are in the process of surrendering and your spiritual friend at that point seems to point his scalpel at you and take away your anaesthesia, then that is an extremely terrifying situation. Your spiritual friend seems to be very angry and disgusted and you want to run. Would you explain this?

A: That is just the point. It is a matter of an operation without the use of anaesthetics. You have to be willing to do it.

If you run away, it is like a man who needs an appendectomy running out of the operating room; his appendix might burst.

Q: But this is at a very early stage in your relationship with your spiritual friend; you have barely been with him for five minutes. Suddenly the roof falls in and he just leaves you to deal with it. Perhaps he is saying, "I am not going on this trip with you. Five minutes have passed. Surrender it, give it all up, deal with it yourself, and when you have cut it all loose, then I will talk to you." That is how I have experienced it.

A: You see, it does not matter whether you are a beginning or advanced student. It is a question of how much a person has been with himself. If he has been with himself, then he must know himself. It is like an ordinary illness. Suppose you are travelling from one country to another and you feel ill and decide to see a doctor. He can barely speak your language, but he can feel your body and see what is wrong with you, and he decides to take you immediately to the hospital and operate. It depends upon how far the disease has developed. The intensity of the operation depends on the maturity of the illness in your body. You might explode completely. If you have appendicitis and the doctor waits too long, perhaps in order to become friends with you, then your appendix is going to explode. You would not say that was a very good way of practicing medicine.

Q: Why does someone take that first step on the path? What leads him to it? Is it an accident, is it fate, karma, what is it?

A: If you expose yourself completely, then you are already on the path. If you give yourself halfway, then you are only part way on the path. It is going to bounce back on you. If you give less information to your doctor, then you are going to recover much more slowly because you have not told him your whole case history. The more you tell your doctor, the sooner he will be able to cure you.

Q: If the truly hard way is to expose myself, then should I allow myself to be exposed to what I judge to be evil, knowing I might get hurt?

A: Opening is not a matter of martyring oneself to every threat that comes along. You do not have to stand in front of an oncoming train to open yourself to it. That would be the way of heroism, the false hard way.

Whenever we confront something we regard as "evil," it poses a threat to the self-preservation of ego. We are so busy preserving our existence in the face of this threat that we cannot see the thing clearly at all. To open we have to cut through our desire to preserve our own existence. Then we can see and deal with the situation clearly, as it is.

Q: This is not a one-shot deal, is it? I mean you can open yourself in one context, and yet when you find yourself in some other situation suddenly you take hold of a mask and put it over your face, even though you really do not want to do it. It would seem that achieving complete openness is a difficult thing.

A: The whole point is that struggle is irrelevant to opening. Once you have stepped on the path, if you give up the struggle itself, that takes care of the whole problem. Then there is no longer any question of wanting or not wanting to be involved with life-situations. The ape instinct of ego dissolves because it is based upon secondhand information rather than upon direct experience of what is. Struggle is ego. Once you give up struggle, then there is no one left to conquer struggle; it just disappears. So you see, it is not a matter of achieving a victory over struggle.

Q: When you feel angry, should you just express that anger in order to open?

A: When we speak of opening and surrendering as, for instance, in the case of anger, it does not mean we should actually go out and hit someone on the spot. That seems to be more a way of feeding ego rather than a way of exposing your anger properly, seeing its real living quality. This applies to exposing yourself in general. It is a matter of seeing the basic quality of the situation, as it is, rather than trying to do something with it. Of course if one is completely open to the situation without any preconceptions, then one would know which action is right and which is unskillful. If a particular course of action would be clumsy and unskilled, then you would not take that fork in the road; you would take the road of skillful and creative action. You are not really involved with judgment as such, but you choose the creative way.

Q: Is collecting things and defending disguises an inescapable stage?

A: We collect things and later it is painful to give them away. It is similar to having stitches in our skin after an operation. It is frightening to have them taken out, we are apprehensive, we have become accustomed to a foreign element in our system.

Q: Do you think it is possible to begin to see what is, to see yourself as you are, without a teacher?

A: I do not think it is possible at all. You have to have a spiritual friend in order to surrender and completely open yourself.

Q: Is it absolutely necessary that the spiritual friend be a living human being?
A: Yes. Any other "being" with whom you might think yourself communicating would be imaginary.

Q: Would the teachings of Christ in themselves be a spiritual friend?
A: I would not say so. That is an imaginary situation. It is the same with any teachings; they do not have to be the teachings of Christ necessarily. The problem is that we can interpret them ourselves. That is the whole point: written teachings are always open to the interpretation of ego.

Q: When you speak of opening and exposing yourself, it reminds me a great deal of certain schools of psychotherapy. What do you think is the function of the sort of things people do in psychotherapy?
A: In most forms of psychotherapy the problem is that, if you regard the process as "therapeutic," then you do not really mean it but it is the therapeutic thing to do. In other words, your therapy is a hobby. Moreover, you see your therapeutic situation as being defined by your case history. Because something went wrong in your relationship with your father and mother, you have this unhealthy tendency to . . . Once you begin to deal with a person's whole case history, trying to make it relevant to the present, the person begins to feel that he has no escape, that his situation is hopeless, because he cannot undo his past. He feels trapped by his past with no way out. This kind of treatment is extremely unskilled. It is

destructive because it hinders involvement with the creative aspect of what is happening now, what is here, right now. But on the other hand, if psychotherapy is presented with the emphasis on living in the present moment, working with present problems, not just as regards verbal expression and thoughts alone but in terms of experiencing the actuality of emotions and feelings, then I think that would be a very balanced style. Unfortunately there are many kinds of psychotherapy and many psychotherapists involved with trying to prove themselves and their own theories rather than working with what is. In fact they find it very frightening to work with what is.

We must simplify rather than complicate the problem with theories of any kind. The situation of nowness, this very moment, contains whole case histories and future determinations. Everything is right here, so we do not have to go any further than this to prove who we were or are or might be. As soon as we try to unravel the past, then we are involved with ambition and struggle in the present, not being able to accept the present moment as it is. It is very cowardly. Moreover, it is unhealthy to regard our therapist or guru as our savior. We must work on ourselves. There is really no other alternative. The spiritual friend might accentuate our pain in certain circumstances. That is part of the physician-patient relationship. The idea is not to regard the spiritual path as something very luxurious and pleasurable but to see it as just facing the facts of life.

The Open Way

It should be clear by now that in order to find the open way we must first experience self-deception as it is, exposing ourselves completely. We may even be hesitant to consider such a hopeful subject as the open way, because we are so wary of our ambition. But our caution is a sign that we are ready to think about it. In fact, hesitation at this point could be another form of self-deception: ignoring the teachings with the rationale of trying to be perfect and extremely careful.

The approach to the open way lies in the experience of exposing oneself—an experience we discussed in the lecture "Initiation"—opening oneself to life, being what you are, presenting your positive and negative qualities to your spiritual friend and working your way through. Then having presented yourself, having experienced initiation, the meeting of the two minds, you might tend to evaluate your credentials. You have experienced such an extraordinary incident; you were able to open, and your spiritual friend opened, and you met both yourself and your spiritual friend in the same moment. It was exciting, beautiful.

The problem lies in the fact that we are always trying to secure ourselves, reassure ourselves that we are all right. We are constantly looking for something solid to hang on to. The "miraculous" situation of the meeting of the two minds is such a fantastic experience that it seems to confirm our expectation of miracles and magic.

So the next step on the path of self-deception is the desire to see miracles. We have read many books describing the lives of great yogis and swamis, saints and avatars. And all these seem to speak of extraordinary miracles. Either someone walked through a wall or someone turned the world upside-down—all these miracles. You would like to prove to yourself that such miracles do exist, because you would like to be sure that you are on the side of the guru, the side of the doctrine, the side of the miracles, sure that what you are doing is safe and powerful, sensational in fact, sure that you are on the side of the "goodies." You would like to be one of those few people who have done something fantastic, extraordinary, super-extraordinary, one of the people who turned the world upside-down: "I actually thought that I was standing on the floor, but I found myself standing on the ceiling!" The sudden flash of the meeting with the spiritual friend, the meeting of the two minds, is definitely real, a genuine experience, quite sensational, a miracle in fact. Perhaps we are not quite *absolutely* sure, but certainly such a miracle must mean that we are on to something, that we have found the true way at last.

Such intense attempts to prove to ourselves that what we are doing is right indicate a very introverted state of mind; one is very aware of oneself and the state of one's being. We feel that we are a minority and that we are doing something very extraordinary, that we are different from everyone else. This sort of attempt to prove our own uniqueness is just an attempt to validate our self-deception. "Of course I experienced something extraordinary; of course I saw the miracle; of course I had the insight; therefore I am going on." Which is a very closed-in, introverted situation. We have no time to relate to anyone else, our friends or relatives, the outside world. We are concerned only with ourselves.

Eventually this approach becomes tedious and stale. We begin to realize that we have been deceiving ourselves and we begin to move closer to the genuine open way. We begin to suspect that all our beliefs are hallucinatory, that we have distorted our experience by evaluating it. "True, I had a flash of instant enlightenment, but at the same time I tried to possess it, grasp it, and it went away." We begin to discover that self-deception does not work at all, that it is simply trying to comfort oneself, trying to contact oneself inwardly, trying to prove something to oneself rather than really being open. At this point one might begin to punish oneself saying, "If I am trying not to deceive myself, then that is another kind of self-deception; and if I try to avoid doing that, then that is self-deception too. How can I possibly free myself? And if I am trying to free myself, then that is another form of self-deception as well," and so the chain reaction goes on and on and on, the chain reaction of overlapping paranoia.

Having discovered self-deception, we suffer from tremendous paranoia and self criticism, which is helpful. It is good to experience the hopelessness of ambition, of trying to be open, of trying to cheer ourselves up, because this prepares the ground for another type of attitude toward spirituality. The whole point we are trying to get to is—when are we going to open, *really?* The action of our mind is so overlapping, an ingrown toenail, introverted: If I do this, then that is going to happen; if I do that, then this is going to happen. How can I escape the self-deception? I recognize it, I see it, but how am I going to get out of it?

I am afraid each of us has to go through this individually.

I am not giving a guided tour to enlightenment. I do not guarantee anything. But I am just suggesting that perhaps there is something wrong with this approach.

Perhaps we do feel that something is wrong with this approach and we seek advice from our guru.

"I am completely convinced that this path is right for me, of course—we do not even have to discuss that. But something seems to be wrong. I have worked and worked on myself, and yet I find myself involved in a chain reaction of overlapping defeats."

"Okay then, what next?"

"Well, I am too busy to do anything else because I am so obsessed with all this."

"Okay, relax yourself."

"What can I do? Haven't you got any suggestions?"

"I am afraid I cannot give you an immediate solution to your problem. I have to know what is actually wrong with you, to start with. That is what all professional people would say. If there is something wrong with your television set, you do not immediately plug in a new tube. First you must examine the entire set. Which part does not function? Which tubes do not work?"

"Well, there doesn't seem to be anything wrong exactly. But the minute I try to touch on the subject it just goes berserk, it doesn't click anymore. When I try to do something to correct it, I get no results at all. Something seems to be fused."

"Big problem."

"You see, each time I try to work my way out, as you and other gurus told me to do, I try and try and try but there doesn't seem to be an end to the problem at all. Things keep going wrong all the time. If I start practicing *asanas, pranayama, zazen,* anything, much as I try to do it correctly, still the same familiar problems come back again and again and again. I have great faith in these doctrines, teachings, methods —of course I do. I love the teachers. I love the methods, I really do. I have complete faith in them. I know that a lot of people turn out beautifully as a result of travelling the same path I am attempting, but what is wrong with me? Maybe I have bad karma, maybe I am the black sheep of the family. Could that be so? If it is so, then I will go on a pilgrimage on my knees to India, I will make any sacrifice needed. I could starve myself. I will take any vow, but I just want to get it, really get into it. What can I do? Isn't there anything else in your sacred books prescribing something appropriate for a person like me? Isn't there some medicine I can take, a sacrifice I can perform?"

"I'm not sure. Come back later tomorrow and see me. Perhaps we can find something."

That is what a spiritual friend might say: "See me again tomorrow or on the weekend. Let's talk it over but don't worry." You go again, you see him, you think that you have some tremendous problem and that he has all the answers worked out especially for you. And again he will ask:

"How are you? How are you getting on?"

"What do you mean? I was waiting for *your* answer. You know how I am—I'm in terrible shape!"

You become very grumpy, and quite rightly in a way. Nothing happens, as usual, and then weeks and weeks go by as you come back again and again and again. You despair, suspecting nothing will come of the whole thing, entertaining the secret wish that maybe this is the time, maybe the fourth week or the fifth week or the seventh week. Seven is very symbolic, a mystic number. Time goes on: complete despair. You are about to investigate the possibility of other solutions.

"Maybe if I go and see someone else," you think. "Perhaps I should return home and work with my own people; this situation is too alien to me. There seems to be no communication between him and me. He is supposed to have some kind of communication with me, but it is very disappointing, nothing happens at all." So you sit and wait. Whenever you see him, you almost immediately know what his words to you are going to be: "Go back and meditate," or "How are you? Have a cup of tea." It is the same thing, again and again.

What is wrong? In fact nothing is wrong at all, absolutely nothing. The situation is quite beautiful, as far as your spiritual friend is concerned. But this period of waiting on your part, trying to get over something, is in itself wrong, because a waiting period means so much concentration into yourself, working inward rather than working outward. There is a tendency towards centralization and there is the notion of the "big deal" involved with your psychology, your state of mind. That is what is wrong.

Perhaps I should tell you the story of Naropa and his teacher Tilopa, the great Indian sage. Tilopa was a guru who spent twelve years with his student Naropa doing practically the same kind of thing we have been discussing here. "If you fetch me soup from that kitchen, I will teach you, I might teach you," Tilopa would say. Then Naropa would bring the soup, having endured a terrible beating at the hands of the kitchen staff and householders in order to get it. He would arrive bloody but happy, and when he had presented the soup, Tilopa would say, "I want another cup, go and fetch it." So Naropa would go and fetch the soup, returning half dead. He did this because he yearned so for the teachings. Then Tilopa would say, "Thank you, let's go somewhere else." This sort of incident occurred again and again until Naropa's sense of expectation had reached its crescendo. At just this point Tilopa took off his sandal and slapped Naropa in the face. That was the abhisheka, the highest and most profound, the greatest— you could use many more adjectives to describe it—the greatest abhisheka. The slapping of a sandal against a man's cheek and suddenly there was nothing more for Naropa to work with.

But we must not get carried away with this mystical scene. The whole point is the open path, the open way. We have thoroughly examined and experienced self-deception. We have been carrying such a heavy burden, like a tortoise carrying its shell. We have continually attempted to seal ourselves into this shell, trying actually to get into "somewhere" with such aggression and speed. We must give up all our speed and aggression, the whole demanding quality. We must develop some compassion for ourselves, and then the open way just begins.

At this point we should discuss the meaning of compassion, which is the key to and the basic atmosphere of the open way. The best and most correct way of presenting the idea of compassion is in terms of clarity, clarity which contains fundamental warmth. At this stage your meditation practice is the act of trusting in yourself. As your practice becomes more prominent in daily life activities, you begin to trust yourself and have a compassionate attitude. Compassion in this sense is not feeling sorry for someone. It is basic warmth. As much space and clarity as there is, there is that much warmth as well, some delightful feeling of positive things happening in yourself constantly. Whatever you are doing, it is not regarded as a mechanical drag in terms of self-conscious meditation, but meditation is a delightful and spontaneous thing to do. It is the continual act of making friends with yourself.

Then, having made friends with yourself, you cannot just

contain that friendship within you; you must have some out-
let, which is your relationship with the world. So compassion
becomes a bridge to the world outside. Trust and compassion
for oneself bring inspiration to dance with life, to communicate with the energies of the world. Lacking this kind of inspiration and openness, the spiritual path becomes the samsaric path of desire. One remains trapped in the desire to
improve oneself, the desire to achieve imagined goals. If we
feel that we cannot achieve our goal, we suffer despair and
the self-torture of unfulfilled ambition. On the other hand, if
we feel that we are succeeding in achieving our goal, we might
become self-satisfied and aggressive. "I know what I'm doing,
don't touch me." We might become bloated with our knowledge, like certain "experts" we meet who know their subject
thoroughly. If anyone asks questions, especially stupid or
challenging questions, they get angry rather than trying to
explain anything. "How could you say such a thing, how could
you even dream of asking such stupid questions? Don't you
see what I know?"

Or we might even succeed at some form of dualistic concentration practice and experience a kind of "mystical state."
In such cases we might appear quite tranquil and religious in
the conventional sense. But we would constantly have to charge
up and maintain our "mystical state" and there would be a
continual sense of appreciation, the repeated act of checking
and indulging in our achievement. This is the typical distortion of the Hinayana practice of self-contained meditation,
self-enlightenment, and it is in some sense a form of aggression. There is no element of compassion and openness because
one is so focused on one's own experience.

Compassion has nothing to do with achievement at all. It is
spacious and very generous. When a person develops real

compassion, he is uncertain whether he is being generous to others or to himself because compassion is environmental generosity, without direction, without "for me" and without "for them." It is filled with joy, spontaneously existing joy, constant joy in the sense of trust, in the sense that joy contains tremendous wealth, richness.

We could say that compassion is the ultimate attitude of wealth: an anti-poverty attitude, a war on want. It contains all sorts of heroic, juicy, positive, visionary, expansive qualities. And it implies larger scale thinking, a freer and more expansive way of relating to yourself and the world. This is precisely why the second *yana* is called the "Mahayana," the "Great Vehicle." It is the attitude that one has been born fundamentally rich rather than that one must become rich. Without this kind of confidence meditation cannot be transferred into action at all.

Compassion automatically invites you to relate with people, because you no longer regard people as a drain on your energy. They recharge your energy, because in the process of relating with them you acknowledge your wealth, your richness. So, if you have difficult tasks to perform, such as dealing with people or life situations, you do not feel you are running out of resources. Each time you are faced with a difficult task it presents itself as a delightful opportunity to demonstrate your richness, your wealth. There is no feeling of poverty at all in this approach to life.

Compassion as the key to the open way, the Mahayana, makes possible the transcendental actions of the *bodhisattva*. The Bodhisattva Path starts with generosity and openness— giving and openness—the surrendering process. Openness is not a matter of giving something to someone else, but it means giving up your demand and the basic criteria of the demand.

This is the *dana paramita*, the paramita of generosity. It is learning to trust in the fact that you do not need to secure your ground, learning to trust in your fundamental richness, that you can afford to be open. This is the open way. If you give up your psychological attitude of "demand," then basic health begins to evolve, which leads to the next act of the bodhisattva, the *shila* paramita, the paramita of morality or discipline.

Having opened, having given up everything without reference to the basic criteria of "I am doing this, I am doing that," without reference to oneself, then other situations connected with maintaining ego or collecting become irrelevant. That is the ultimate morality and it intensifies the situation of openness and bravery: you are not afraid of hurting yourself or anyone else because you are completely open. You do not feel uninspired with situations, which brings patience, the *kshanti* paramita. And patience leads to energy, *virya*—the quality of delight. There is the tremendous joy of involvement, which is energy, which also brings the panoramic vision of open meditation—the experience of *dhyana*—openness. You do not regard the situation outside as separate from you because you are so involved with the dance and play of life.

Then you become even more open. You do not regard anything as being rejected or accepted; you are just going along with each situation. You experience no warfare of any kind, neither trying to defeat an enemy nor trying to achieve a goal. There is no involvement with collecting or giving. No hope or fear at all. This is the development of *prajna*, transcendent knowledge, the ability to see situations as they are.

So the main theme of the open way is that we must begin to abandon the basic struggle of ego. To be completely open, to have that kind of absolute trust in yourself is the real meaning of compassion and love. There have been so many speeches about love and peace and tranquility in the world. But how do we really bring love into being? Christ said, "Love thy neighbor," but how do we love? How do we do it? How are we going to radiate our love to the whole of humanity, to the whole world? "Because we must, and that's the truth!" "If you don't love, you are condemned, evil; you are doing a disservice to humanity." "If you love, you are on the path, you are on the right track." But how? Many people get very romantic about love, in fact get high on it at the very word. But then there will be a gap, a period when we are not high on love. Something else takes place which is embarrassing, a private matter. We tend to seal it off; it is "private parts," shameful, not part of our divinity. Let's not think about that. Let's simply ignite another love explosion and on and on we go, trying to ignore those parts of our being we reject, trying to be virtuous, loving, kind.

Perhaps this will put off a lot of people, but I am afraid love is not really the experience of beauty and romantic joy alone. Love is associated with ugliness and pain and aggression, as well as with the beauty of the world; it is not the recreation of heaven. Love or compassion, the open path, is associated with "what is." In order to develop love—universal love, cosmic love, whatever you would like to call it—one must accept the whole situation of life as it is, both the light and the dark, the good and the bad. One must open oneself to life, communicate with it. Perhaps you are fighting to develop love and peace, struggling to achieve them: "We are going to make it, we are going to spend thousands of dollars in order to broadcast the doctrine of love everywhere, we are going to proclaim love." Okay, proclaim it, do it, spend your money, but what about the speed and aggression behind what you are doing? Why do you have to push us into the accep-

tance of your love? Why is there such speed and force involved? If your love is moving with the same speed and drive
as other people's hatred, then something appears to be wrong.
It would seem to be the same as calling darkness light. There
is so much ambition involved, taking the form of proselytizing.
It is not an open situation of communication with things as
they are. The ultimate implication of the words "peace on
earth" is to remove altogether the ideas of peace and war and
to open yourself equally and completely to the positive and
negative aspects of the world. It is like seeing the world from
an aerial point of view: there is light, there is dark; both are
accepted. You are not trying to defend the light against the
dark.

The action of the bodhisattva is like the moon shining on
one hundred bowls of water, so that there are one hundred
moons, one in each bowl. This is not the moon's design nor
was it designed by anyone else. But for some strange reason
there happen to be one hundred moons reflected in one hundred bowls of water. Openness means this kind of absolute
trust and self-confidence. The open situation of compassion
works this way rather than by deliberately attempting to
create one hundred moons, one in each bowl.

The basic problem we seem to be facing is that we are too
involved with trying to prove something, which is connected
with paranoia and the feeling of poverty. When you are trying to prove or get something, you are not open anymore, you
have to check everything, you have to arrange it "correctly."
It is such a paranoid way to live and it really does not prove
anything. One might set records in terms of numbers and
quantities—that we have built the greatest, the biggest, we
have collected the most, the longest, the most gigantic. But

who is going to remember the record when you are dead? Or
in one hundred years? Or in ten years? Or in ten minutes?
The records that count are those of the given moment, of now
—whether or not communication and openness are actually
taking place now.

This is the open way, the Bodhisattva Path. A bodhisattva
would not care, even if he received a medal from all the Buddhas proclaiming him the bravest bodhisattva in the entire
universe; he would not care at all. You never read stories of
the bodhisattvas receiving medals in the sacred writings. And
quite rightly so, because there is no need for them to prove
anything. The bodhisattva's action is spontaneous, it is the
open life, open communication which does not involve struggle
or speed at all.

Q: I assume that being a bodhisattva means helping people,
and people make specific demands. So a bodhisattva must perform specific acts. But how does this idea of being totally open
fit in with the need to perform specific acts?
A: Being open does not mean being unresponsive, a zombie.
It means being free to do whatever is called for in a given
situation. Because you do not want anything from the situation, you are free to act in the way genuinely appropriate to
it. And, similarly, if other people want something from you,
that may be their problem. You do not have to try to ingratiate
yourself with anyone. Openness means "being what you are."
If you are comfortable being yourself, then an environment
of openness and communication arises automatically and naturally. It is like the idea of the moon and the bowls of water
which we have been discussing: if the bowls are there, they
will reflect your "moonness." If they are not there, they will

not. Or if they are only half there, then they will reflect only half a moon. It is up to them. You are just there, the moon, open, and the bowls may reflect you or not. You neither care nor do you not care. You are just there.

Situations develop automatically. We do not need to fit ourselves into special roles and environments. I think many of us have been trying to do that for a long time, limiting ourselves, pigeonholing ourselves into narrowly defined sets of circumstances. We spend so much energy focusing our attention in just one place that to our surprise we discover that there are whole areas we have missed.

Q: Can one act with compassion and still get things done as they need to be done?
A: When there is no speed or aggression, you feel that there is room enough in which to move about and do things and you see the things which need to be done more clearly. You become more efficient and your work becomes more precise.

Q: I believe, Rinpoche, that you made a distinction between the open path and the internal path. Could you amplify what differences you see between the internal and the external?
A: Well, the word "internal," as you are using it, seems to imply struggle, turning back into yourself, considering whether or not you are a sufficiently worthy, functional and presentable person. In this approach there is too much "working on oneself," too much concentration inward. Whereas the open path is a matter of working purely with what is, of giving up altogether the fear that something may not work, that something may end in failure. One has to give up the paranoia that one might not fit into situations, that one might be rejected. One purely deals with life as it is.

Q: Where does the attitude of warmth come from?

A: It comes from the absence of aggression.

Q: But isn't that the goal?

A: As well as the path, the bridge. You do not live on the
bridge. You walk over the bridge. In the experience of meditation there is automatically some sense of the absence of
aggression, which is the definition of dharma. Dharma is defined as "dispassion" or "passionlessness," and passionlessness implies absence of aggression. If you are passionate, you
want to get something quickly to satisfy your desire. When
there is no desire to satisfy yourself, there is no aggression or
speed. So if a person can really relate to the simplicity of the
practice of meditation, then automatically there is an absence
of aggression. Because there is no rush to achieve, you can
afford to relax. Because you can afford to relax, you can afford
to keep company with yourself, can afford to make love with
yourself, be friends with yourself. Then thoughts, emotions,
whatever occurs in the mind constantly accentuates the act of
making friends with yourself.

Another way to put it is to say that compassion is the earthy
quality of meditation practice, the feeling of earth and solidity. The message of compassionate warmth is to not be hasty
and to relate to each situation as it is. The American Indian
name "Sitting Bull" seems to be a perfect example of this.
"Sitting Bull" is very solid and organic. You are really definitely present, resting.

Q: You seemed to say that compassion grows, but it was implied that you do not have to cultivate it.

A: It develops, grows, ferments by itself. It does not need
any effort.

Q: Does it die?

A: It does not seem to die. Shantideva says that every un-compassionate action is like planting a dead tree, but any-thing related to compassion is like planting a living tree. It grows and grows endlessly and never dies. Even if it seems to die, it always leaves behind a seed from which another grows. Compassion is organic; it continues on and on and on.

Q: There is a certain kind of warmth that comes when you start to relate with someone, and then somehow that energy becomes overwhelming and catches you up in such a way that there is no longer any space or room to move.

A: If the warmth is without implication and self-reassur-ance, then it is self-sustaining and fundamentally healthy. When you make yoghurt, if you raise the temperature or try to nurse the yoghurt more than necessary, you do not make good yoghurt at all. If you leave it at the right temperature and just abandon it, it will be good yoghurt.

Q: How do you know when to abandon it?

A: You do not constantly have to manage yourself. You must disown rather than attempt to maintain control, trust yourself rather than check yourself. The more you try to check yourself, the greater the possibility of interrupting the natural play and growth of the situation. Even if what you are doing is chancy, even if it seems possible that the whole affair will blow up and become distorted, you do not worry about it.

Q: What happens when someone creates a situation and you do worry about it?

A: Worrying does not help at all. In fact it makes things worse.

Q: It seems the process we are talking about requires some sort of fearlessness.
A: Yes, very much so. It is positive thinking, the mentality of wealth.

Q: What if you feel the necessity for a violent act in order ultimately to do good for a person?
A: You just do it.

Q: But if you are not at that point of true compassion and wisdom?
A: You do not question or worry about your wisdom. You just do whatever is required. The situation you are facing is itself profound enough to be regarded as knowledge. You do not need secondary resources of information. You do not need reinforcement or guidelines for action. Reinforcement is provided by the situation automatically. When things must be conducted in a tough manner, you just do it because the situation demands your response. You do not impose toughness; you are an instrument of the situation.

Q: What do you do for a bridge when you don't feel compassionate?
A: You do not have to *feel* compassion. That is the distinction between emotional compassion and *compassion* compassion: you do not necessarily feel it; you *are* it. Usually, if you are open, compassion happens because you are not preoccupied with some kind of self-indulgence.

Q: Does the bridge of compassion require continual maintenance?

A: I do not think so. It requires acknowledgement rather than maintenance. That is the mentality of wealth; that you acknowledge that the bridge is there.

Q: What do you do when you are afraid of someone, perhaps with reason? For me, this destroys compassion.

A: Compassion is not looking down upon somebody who needs help, who needs care, but it is general, basic, organic, positive thinking. The fear of someone else seems to generate uncertainty as to who you are. That is why you are afraid of that particular situation or person. Fear comes from uncertainty. If you know exactly how you are going to handle this frightful situation, then you have no fear. Fear comes from panic, the bewilderment of uncertainty. Uncertainty is related to distrust in yourself, feeling that you are inadequate to deal with that mysterious problem which is threatening you. There is no fear if you really have a compassionate relationship with yourself, because then you know what you are doing. If you know what you are doing, then your projections also become methodical or predictable, in some sense. Then one develops *prajna*, knowledge of how to relate to any given situation.

Q: What do you mean by projections in this context?

A: Projection is the mirror reflection of yourself. Because you are uncertain about yourself, the world reflects that uncertainty back to you and the reflection begins to haunt you. Your uncertainty is haunting you, but it is merely your reflection in the mirror.

Q: What do you mean by saying that, if you are compas-

sionate towards yourself, then you know what you are doing?
A: These two aspects of meditation always appear simultaneously. If you are opening to yourself and have a positive
attitude towards yourself, then automatically you know what
you are doing because you are not a mystery to yourself. This
is *jnana,* "wisdom," "spontaneously-existing-awareness-wis-
dom." You know that you are spontaneously existing, you
know what you are, therefore you can afford to trust yourself
at the same time.

Q: If I really were to make friends with myself, then I
wouldn't be afraid of making mistakes all the time?
A: That's it. The Tibetan word for wisdom is *yeshe,* which
means "primordial intelligence." You are yourself at the beginning of any beginning. You could almost call it "unorig-
inated trust in yourself." You do not have to find the beginning
at all. It is a primordial situation, so there is no point in trying to logically find the beginning. It *is* already. It is begin-
ningless.

Sense of Humor

It would be interesting to examine this subject in terms of what is *not* a sense of humor. Lack of humor seems to come from the attitude of the "hard fact." Things are very hard and deadly honest, deadly serious, like, to use an analogy, a living corpse. He lives in pain, has a continual expression of pain on his face. He has experienced some kind of hard fact —"reality"—he is deadly serious and has gone so far as to become a living corpse. The rigidity of this living corpse expresses the opposite of a sense of humor. It is as though somebody is standing behind you with a sharp sword. If you are not meditating properly, sitting still and upright, there will be someone behind you just about to strike. Or if you are not dealing with life properly, honestly, directly, someone is just about to hit you. This is the self-consciousness of watching yourself, observing yourself unnecessarily. Whatever we do is constantly being watched and censored. Actually it is not Big Brother who is watching; it is Big Me! Another aspect of me is watching me, behind me, just about to strike, just about to pinpoint my failure. There is no joy in this approach, no sense of humor at all.

This kind of seriousness relates to the problem of spiritual materialism as well. "Inasmuch as I am part of a particular

lineage of meditators, associated with the church and its organization, because of my religious commitment, I must be
a good boy or girl, an honest, good, church-going person. I
must conform to the standards of the church, its rules and
regulations. If I do not fulfill my obligations I will be condemned, reduced to a shrunken body." There is the threat of
solemnity and death—death in the sense of an end to any
further creative process. This attitude has the feeling of limitation, rigidity; there is no room to move about at all.

You might ask then, "What about the great religious traditions, the teachings? They speak of discipline, rules and regulations. How do we reconcile these with the notion of a sense
of humor?" Well, let's examine the question properly. Are
the regulations, the discipline, the practice of morality really
based on the purely judgmental attitude of "good" as opposed
to "bad"? Are the great spiritual teachings really advocating
that we fight evil because we are on the side of light, the side
of peace? Are they telling us to fight against that other "undesirable" side, the bad and the black? That is a big question.
If there is wisdom in the sacred teachings, there should not
be any war. As long as a person is involved with warfare,
trying to defend or attack, then his action is not sacred; it is
mundane, dualistic, a battlefield situation. One would not
expect the great teachings to be as simple-minded as that, trying to be good, fighting the bad. Such would be the approach
of the Hollywood western movie—even before you have seen
the conclusion, you already know precisely that the "goodies"
will not be killed and the "baddies" are going to get smashed.
This approach is obviously simple-minded; but it is just this
type of situation that we are creating in terms of "spiritual"
struggle, "spiritual" achievement.

I am not saying that a sense of humor should be wildly unleashed. I am speaking of seeing something more than just warfare, struggle, duality. If we regard the path of spirituality as a battlefield, then we are weak and feeble. Then our progress on the path will depend upon how great an area we have conquered, upon the subjugation of our own and others' faults, upon how much negativity we have eliminated. Relative to how much dark you have eliminated; that much light you have been able to produce. That is very feeble; one could hardly call it liberation or freedom or *mukti* or *nirvana*. You have achieved liberation by defeating something else: it is purely relative.

I do not want to make a "sense of humor" into something solemn; I am afraid that people are going to do that. But in order to really understand rigidity, that which is represented by the corpse, one cannot avoid the danger of making a sense of humor into a serious thing. Sense of humor means seeing both poles of a situation as they are, from an aerial point of view. There is good and there is bad and you see both with a panoramic view as though from above. Then you begin to feel that these little people on the ground, killing each other or making love or just being little people, are very insignificant in the sense that, if they begin to make a big deal of their warfare or love making, then we begin to see the ironic aspect of their clamor. If we try very hard to build something tremendous, really meaningful, powerful—"I'm really searching for something, I'm really trying to fight my faults," or "I'm really trying to be good,"—then it loses its seriousness, becomes a paper tiger; it is extremely ironic.

Sense of humor seems to come from all-pervading joy, joy which has room to expand into a completely open situation because it is not involved with the battle between "this" and "that". Joy develops into the panoramic situation of seeing or feeling the whole ground, the open ground. This open situation has no hint of limitation, of imposed solemnity. And if you do try to treat life as a "serious business," if you try to impose solemnity upon life as though everything is a big deal, then it is funny. Why such a big deal?

A person might attempt to meditate in a 100% or 200% correct posture. Big Deal. Funny. Or on the other hand, a person might try to develop a sense of humor, trying always to make fun of things, to find humor in every corner, every crack. That in itself is a very serious game, which is equally funny. If you build up physical tension to the point where you are clenching your teeth, biting your tongue, then suddenly something will tickle you because you have been building too much; it is too absurd to go to such extremes. That extreme intensity itself becomes humor, automatically.

There is the Tibetan story of a certain monk who renounced his samsaric, confused life and decided to go live in a cave in order to meditate all the time. Prior to this he had been thinking continually of pain and suffering. His name was Ngonagpa of Langru, the Black-faced One of Langru, because he never smiled at all but saw everything in life in terms of pain. He remained in retreat for many years, very solemn and deadly honest, until one day he looked at the shrine and saw that someone had presented a big lump of turquoise as a gift to him. As he viewed the gift, he saw a mouse creep in and try to drag away the piece of turquoise. The mouse could not do it, so it sent back to its hole and called another mouse. They both tried to drag away this big lump of turquoise but could not do it. So they squeaked together and called eight more mice who came and finally managed to drag the whole lump back into their hole. Then for the first time Ngonagpa of

Langru began to laugh and smile. And that was his first introduction to openness, a sudden flash of enlightenment.

So a sense of humor is not merely a matter of trying to tell
jokes or make puns, trying to be funny in a deliberate fashion.
It involves seeing the basic irony of the juxtaposition of extremes, so that one is not caught taking them seriously, so
that one does not seriously play their game of hope and fear.
This is why the experience of the spiritual path is so significant, why the practice of meditation is the most insignificant
experience of all. It is insignificant because you place no value
judgment on it. Once you are absorbed into that insignificant
situation of openness without involvement in value judgment,
then you begin to see all the games going on around you.
Someone is trying to be stern and spiritually solemn, trying
to be a good person. Such a person might take it seriously if
someone offended him, might want to fight. If you work in
accordance with the basic insignificance of what is, then you
begin to see the humor in this kind of solemnity, in people
making such a big deal about things.

Q: Most of the arguments I've heard for doing the good
thing and the right thing say: First accumulate merit, be good,
give up evil; then later on it will be even easier to give up the
"good hang-ups." What do you make of this approach?
A: If we look at it from the point of view of a sense of humor, the idea of "giving up" seems to be too literal and naive.
If you are attempting to be good and give up everything,
ironically it is not giving up at all; it is taking on more things.
That is the funny part of it. Someone might think himself able
to abandon the big load he is carrying but the absence of the
load, the giving up, is heavier, hundreds of times heavier than

what the person has left behind. It is easy to give something up but the by-product of such renunciation could consist of some very heavy virtue. Each time you meet someone you will be thinking or will actually say, "I have given up this and that." "Giving up" can become heavier and heavier, as though you were carrying a big bag of germs on your back. Finally it might become a big fungus that you are carrying, growing faster and faster. At some stage a person begins to become completely unbearable because he has given up so many things.

For that matter, if we treat the practice of meditation as a serious matter, a matter of consequence, then it will become embarrassing and heavy, overwhelming. We will not even be able to think about it. It would be as though a person had eaten an extremely heavy meal. He is just about to get sick and he will begin to think, "I wish I were hungry. At least that would feel light. But now I have all this food in my sto- mach and I am just about to be sick. I wish I had never eaten." One cannot take spirituality so seriously. It is self-defeating, counter to the true meaning of "giving up."

Q: Is a sense of tragedy then something that an enlightened person has overcome?
A: You do not necessarily have to be enlightened to give up tragedy. If you are involved with the intensity of crescendo situations, with the intensity of tragedy, then you might begin to see the humor of these situations as well. As in music, when we hear the crescendo building, suddenly if the music stops, we begin to hear the silence as part of the music. It is not an extraordinary experience at all: it is very ordinary, very mun- dane. That is why I said it is one of the most insignificant ex- periences of all, because we do not attach our value judgments

to it. The experience is hardly there. Of course if we employ the basic twist of ego, we could go on and say that because the experience is hardly there, because it is so insignificant, therefore it is one of the most valuable and extraordinary experiences of all. This would just be a conceptualized way of trying to prove that what you are involved in is a big deal. It is *not* a big deal.

Q: Is sense of humor related in any way to the experience of instant enlightenment, *satori*?

A: Certainly. There is the story of a person who died laughing. He was a simple village person who asked a teacher the color of Amitabha which traditionally, iconographically, is red. Somehow, by mistake, he thought the teacher said Amitabha's color was the color of ash in a fire. And this influenced his whole meditation practice; because when he practiced visualizing Amitabha, it was a grey Amitabha.

Finally the man was dying. As he lay on his deathbed he wanted to make sure, so he asked another teacher the color of Amitabha. The teacher said that Amitabha's color was red and the man suddenly burst into laughter: "Well, I used to think him the color of ash, and now you tell me he is red." He burst into laughter and died laughing. So it is a question of overcoming some kind of seriousness.

There are many stories of people who were actually able to see the awakened state by breaking into laughter—seeing the contrast, the irony of polar situations. For instance there was the hermit whose devotee lived several miles away in a village. This devotee supported the hermit, supplying him with food and the other necessities of life. Most of the time the devotee sent his wife or daughter or son to bring the hermit his supplies; but one day the hermit heard that the donor himself was coming to see him. The hermit thought, "I must impress him, I must clean and polish the shrine objects and make the shrine very neat and my room extremely tidy." So he cleaned and rearranged everything until his shrine looked very impressive with bowls of water and butter lamps burning brightly. And when he had finished, he sat down and began to admire the room and look around. Everything looked very neat, somehow unreal, and he saw that his shrine appeared unreal as well. Suddenly, to his surprise he realized that he was being a hypocrite. Then he went into the kitchen and got hand-fulls of ashes and threw them at the shrine until his room was a complete mess. When his patron came, he was extremely impressed by the natural quality of the room, by its not being tidy. The hermit could not hold himself together. He burst into laughter and said, "I tried to tidy myself and my room, but then I thought perhaps I should show it to you this way." And so they both, patron and hermit, burst into laughter. That was a great moment of awakening for both of them.

Q: In each lecture you describe some seemingly inescapable situation in which we are all trapped, in which we have already become enmeshed. I just wonder if you ever mean to imply that there is a way out?

A: You see, the whole point is that if we are speaking of a way out all the time, then we are dealing in fantasy, the dream of escape, salvation, enlightenment. We need to be practical. We must examine what is here, now, our neurotic mind. Once we are completely familiar with the negative aspects of the state of our being, then we know the "way out" automatically. But if we talk about how beautiful and joyous our attainment of the goal will be, then we become extremely sincere and romantic; and this approach becomes an obstacle.

One must be practical. It is like visiting your physician because you are ill. If a doctor is going to treat you, then he must first know what is wrong with you. It is not a question of what could be right with you; that is not relevant. If you tell the doctor what is wrong with you, then that is the way out of your illness. That is why the Buddha taught the Four Noble Truths, his first teaching. One must begin with the realization of pain, *duhkha*, suffering. Then having realized duhkha, one goes on to the origin of suffering and the path leading out of suffering and liberation. The Buddha did not begin by teaching the beauty of the enlightenment experience.

Q: Following the usual patterns of evaluation and judgment, I find myself thinking that the errors and obstacles which you describe in later lectures are somehow more advanced than those described in the earlier lectures. Is this correct?

A: That is true. Even after one has stepped onto the path, as in the case of bodhisattvas, once you have begun to awaken there could be a tendency to analyze your awakened state. This involves looking at oneself, analyzing and evaluating, and continues until there is a sharp blow which is called the *vajra-like samadhi*. This is the last samadhi state of meditation. The attainment of enlightenment is called "vajra-like" because it does not stand for any nonsense; it just cuts right through all our games. In the story of the Buddha's life we hear of the temptations of Mara, which are extremely subtle. The first temptation is fear of physical destruction. The last is the seduction by the daughters of Mara. This seduction, the seduction of spiritual materialism, is extremely powerful because it is the seduction of thinking that "I" have achieved something. If we think we have achieved something, that we have "made it," then we have been seduced by Mara's daughters, the seduction of spiritual materialism.

The Development of Ego

As we are going to examine the Buddhist path from beginning to end, from the beginner's mind to the enlightened one, I think it would be best to start with something very concrete and realistic, the field we are going to cultivate. It would be foolish to study more advanced subjects before we are familiar with the starting point, the nature of ego. We have a saying in Tibet that, before the head has been cooked properly, grabbing the tongue is of no use. Any spiritual practice needs this basic understanding of the starting point, the material with which we are working.

If we do not know the material with which we are working, then our study is useless; speculations about the goal become mere fantasy. These speculations may take the form of advanced ideas and descriptions of spiritual experiences, but they only exploit the weaker aspects of human nature, our expectations and desires to see and hear something colorful, something extraordinary. If we begin our study with these dreams of extraordinary, "enlightening" and dramatic experiences, then we will build up our expectations and preconceptions so that later, when we are actually working on the path, our minds will be occupied largely with what *will be* rather than with what *is*. It is destructive and not fair to people to play on their weaknesses, their expectations and dreams, rather than to present the realistic starting point of what they are.

It is necessary, therefore, to start on what we are and why we are searching. Generally, all religious traditions deal with this material, speaking variously of *alaya-vijnana* or original sin or the fall of man or the basis of ego. Most religions refer to this material in a somewhat pejorative way, but I do not think it is such a shocking or terrible thing. We do not have to be ashamed of what we are. As sentient beings we have wonderful backgrounds. These backgrounds may not be particularly enlightened or peaceful or intelligent. Nevertheless, we have soil good enough to cultivate; we can plant anything in it. Therefore, in dealing with this subject we are not condemning or attempting to eliminate our ego-psychology; we are purely acknowledging it, seeing it as it is. In fact, the understanding of ego is the foundation of Buddhism. So let us look at how ego develops.

Fundamentally there is just open space, the *basic ground*, what we really are. Our most fundamental state of mind, before the creation of ego, is such that there is basic openness, basic freedom, a spacious quality; and we have now and have always had this openness. Take, for example, our everyday lives and thought patterns. When we see an object, in the first instant there is a sudden perception which has no logic or conceptualization to it at all; we just perceive the thing in the open ground. Then immediately we panic and begin to rush about trying to add something to it, either trying to find a name for it or trying to find pigeon-holes in which we could locate and categorize it. Gradually things develop from there.

This development does not take the shape of a solid entity.

Rather, this development is illusory, the mistaken belief in a "self" or "ego." Confused mind is inclined to view itself as a solid, on-going thing, but it is only a collection of tendencies, events. In Buddhist terminology this collection is referred to as the Five Skandhas or Five Heaps. So perhaps we could go through the whole development of the Five Skandhas.

The beginning point is that there is open space, belonging to no one. There is always primordial intelligence connected with the space and openness. *Vidya*, which means "intelligence" in Sanskrit—precision, sharpness, sharpness with space, sharpness with room in which to put things, exchange things. It is like a spacious hall where there is room to dance about, where there is no danger of knocking things over or tripping over things, for there is completely open space. We *are* this space, we are *one* with it, with vidya, intelligence and openness.

But if we are this all the time, where did the confusion come from, where has the space gone, what has happened? Nothing has happened, as a matter of fact. We just became too active in that space. Because it is spacious, it brings inspiration to dance about; but our dance became a bit too active, we began to spin more than was necessary to express the space. At this point we became *self*-conscious, conscious that "I" am dancing in the space.

At such a point, space is no longer space as such. It becomes solid. Instead of being one with the space, we feel solid space as a separate entity, as tangible. This is the first experience of duality—space and I, I am dancing in this space, and this spaciousness is a solid, separate thing. Duality means "space and I," rather than being completely one with the space. This is the birth of "form," of "other."

Then a kind of blackout occurs, in the sense that we forget what we were doing. There is a sudden halt, a pause; and we turn around and "discover" solid space, as though we had never before done anything at all, as though we were not the creators of all that solidity. There is a gap. Having already created solidified space, then we are overwhelmed by it and begin to become lost in it. There is a blackout and then, suddenly, an awakening.

When we awaken, we refuse to see the space as openness, refuse to see its smooth and ventilating quality. We completely ignore it, which is called *avidya*. *A* means "negation," *vidya* means "intelligence," so it is "un-intelligence." Because this extreme intelligence has been transformed into the perception of solid space, because this intelligence with a sharp and precise and flowing luminous quality has become static, therefore it is called avidya, "ignorance." We deliberately ignore. We are not satisfied just to dance in the space but we want to have a partner, and so we choose the space as our partner. If you choose space as your partner in the dance, then of course you want it to dance with you. In order to possess it as a partner, you have to solidify it and ignore its flowing, open quality. This is avidya, ignorance, ignoring the intelligence. It is the culmination of the First Skandha, the creation of Ignorance-Form.

In fact, this skandha, the skandha of Ignorance-Form, has three different aspects or stages which we could examine through the use of another metaphor. Suppose in the beginning there is an open plain without any mountains or trees, completely open land, a simple desert without any particular characteristics. That is how we are, what we are. We are very simple and basic. And yet there is a sun shining, a moon shining, and there will be lights and colors, the texture of the desert. There will be some feeling of the energy which plays between heaven and earth. This goes on and on.

Then, strangely, there is suddenly someone to notice all this. It is as if one of the grains of sand had stuck its neck out and begun to look around. We are that grain of sand, coming to the conclusion of our separateness. This is the "Birth of Ignorance" in its first stage, a kind of chemical reaction. Duality has begun.

The second stage of Ignorance-Form is called "The Ignorance Born Within." Having noticed that one is separate, then there is the feeling that one has always been so. It is an awkwardness, the instinct toward self-consciousness. It is also one's excuse for remaining separate, an individual grain of sand. It is an aggressive type of ignorance, though not exactly aggressive in the sense of anger; it has not developed as far as that. Rather it is aggression in the sense that one feels awkward, unbalanced, and so one tries to secure one's ground, create a shelter for oneself. It is the attitude that one is a confused and separate individual, and that is all there is to it. One has identified oneself as separate from the basic landscape of space and openness.

The third type of ignorance is "Self-Observing Ignorance," watching oneself. There is a sense of seeing oneself as an external object, which leads to the first notion of "other." One is beginning to have a relationship with a so-called "external" world. This is why these three stages of ignorance constitute the Skandha of Form-Ignorance; one is beginning to create the world of forms.

When we speak of "ignorance" we do not mean stupidity at all. In a sense, ignorance is very intelligent, but it is a completely two-way intelligence. That is to say, one purely reacts to one's projections rather than just seeing what is. There is no situation of "letting be" at all, because one is ignoring what one is all the time. That is the basic definition of ignorance.

The next development is the setting up of a defense mechanism to protect our ignorance. This defense mechanism is Feeling, the Second Skandha. Since we have already ignored open space, we would like next to feel the qualities of solid space in order to bring complete fulfillment to the grasping quality we are developing. Of course space does not mean just bare space, for it contains color and energy. There are tremendous, magnificent displays of color and energy, beautiful and picturesque. But we have ignored them altogether. Instead there is just a solidified version of that color; and the color becomes captured color, and the energy becomes captured energy, because we have solidified the whole space and turned it into "other." So we begin to reach out and feel the qualities of "other." By doing this we reassure ourselves that we exist. "If I can feel that out there, then I must be here."

Whenever anything happens, one reaches out to feel whether the situation is seductive or threatening or neutral. Whenever there is a sudden separation, a feeling of not knowing the relationship of "that" to "this," we tend to feel for our ground. This is the extremely efficient feeling mechanism that we begin to set up, the Second Skandha.

The next mechanism to further establish ego is the Third Skandha, Perception-Impulse. We begin to be fascinated by our own creation, the static colors and the static energies. We want to relate to them, and so we begin gradually to explore our creation.

In order to explore efficiently there must be a kind of switchboard system, a controller of the feeling mechanism. Feeling transmits its information to the central switchboard, which is the act of perception. According to that information, we make judgments, we react. Whether we should react for or against or indifferently is automatically determined by this bureaucracy of feeling and perception. If we feel the situation and find it threatening, then we will push it away from us. If we find it seductive, then we will draw it to us. If we find it neutral, we will be indifferent. These are the three types of impulse: hatred, desire, and stupidity. Thus perception refers to receiving information from the outside world and impulse refers to our response to that information.

The next development is the Fourth Skandha, Concept. Perception-Impulse is an automatic reaction to intuitive feeling. However, this kind of automatic reaction is not really enough of a defense to protect one's ignorance and guarantee one's security. In order to really protect and deceive oneself completely, properly, one needs intellect, the ability to name and categorize things. Thus we label things and events as being "good," "bad," "beautiful," "ugly," and so on, according to which impulse we find appropriate to them.

So the structure of ego is gradually becoming heavier and heavier, stronger and stronger. Up to this point ego's development has been purely an action and reaction process; but from now on ego gradually develops beyond the ape instinct and becomes more sophisticated. We begin to experience intellectual speculation, confirming or interpreting ourselves, putting ourselves into certain logical, interpretive situations. The basic nature of intellect is quite logical. Obviously there will be the tendency to work for a positive condition: to confirm our experience, to interpret weakness into strength, to fabricate a logic of security, to confirm our ignorance.

In a sense, it might be said that the primordial intelligence is operating all the time, but it is being employed by the dualistic fixation, ignorance. In the beginning stages of the development of ego this intelligence operates as the intuitive sharpness of feeling. Later it operates in the form of intellect. Actually it seems that there is no such thing as the ego at all; there is no such thing as "I am." It is an accumulation of a lot of stuff. It is a "brilliant work of art," a product of the intellect which says, "Let's give it a name, let's call it something, let's call it 'I am'," which is very clever. "I" is the product of intellect, the label which unifies into one whole the disorganized and scattered development of ego.

The last stage of the development of ego is the Fifth Skandha, Consciousness. At this level an amalgamation takes place: the intuitive intelligence of the Second Skandha, the energy of the Third, and the intellectualization of the Fourth combine to produce thoughts and emotions. Thus at the level of the Fifth Skandha we find the Six Realms as well as the uncontrollable and illogical patterns of discursive thought.

This is the complete picture of ego. It is in this state that all of us have arrived at our study of Buddhist psychology and meditation.

In Buddhist literature there is a metaphor commonly used to describe this whole process, the creation and development of ego. It speaks of a monkey locked in an empty house, a house with five windows representing the five senses. This monkey is inquisitive, poking its head out of each window and jumping up and down, up and down, restlessly. He is a captive monkey in an empty house. It is a solid house, rather than the jungle in which the monkey leapt and swung, rather than the trees in which he could hear the wind moving and the rustling of the leaves and branches. All these things have become completely solidified. In fact, the jungle itself has become his solid house, his prison. Instead of perching in a tree, this inquisitive monkey has been walled in by a solid world, as if a flowing thing, a dramatic and beautiful waterfall, had suddenly been frozen. This frozen house, made of frozen colors and energies, is completely still. This seems to be the point where time begins as past, future and present. The flux of things becomes solid tangible time, a solid idea of time.

The inquisitive monkey awakens from his blackout, but he does not awaken completely. He awakens to find himself trapped inside of a solid, claustrophobic house with just five windows. He becomes bored, as though captured in a zoo behind iron bars, and he tries to explore the bars by climbing up and down. That he has been captured is not particularly important; but the idea of capture is magnified a thousand times because of his fascination with it. If one is fascinated, the sense of claustrophobia becomes more and more vivid, more and more acute, because one begins to explore one's imprisonment. In fact fascination is part of the reason he remains imprisoned. He is captured by his fascination. Of course at the beginning there was the sudden blackout which confirmed his belief in a solid world. But now having taken solidity for granted, he is trapped by his involvement with it.

Of course this inquisitive monkey does not explore all the time. He begins to become agitated, begins to feel that something is very repetitive and uninteresting, and he begins to become neurotic. Hungry for entertainment, he tries to feel and appreciate the texture of the wall, attempting to make sure that this seeming solidity is really solid. Then, assured that the space is solid, the monkey begins to relate to it by grasping it, repelling it or ignoring it. If he attempts to grasp the space in order to possess it as his own experience, his own discovery, his own understanding, this is desire. Or, if the space seems a prison to him so that he tries to kick and batter his way out, fighting harder and harder, then this is hatred. Hatred is not just the mentality of destruction alone; but it is even more a feeling of defensiveness, defending oneself against claustrophobia. The monkey does not necessarily feel that there is an opponent or enemy approaching; he simply wants to escape his prison.

Finally the monkey might try to ignore that he is imprisoned or that there is something seductive in his environment. He plays deaf and dumb and so is indifferent and slothful in relation to what is happening around him. This is stupidity.

To go back a bit, you might say that the monkey is born into his house as he awakens from the blackout. He does not know how he arrived in this prison, so he assumes he has always been there, forgetting that he himself solidified the space into walls. Then he feels the texture of the walls, which is the Second Skandha, Feeling. After that, he relates to the house in terms of desire, hatred, and stupidity, the Third Skandha, Perception-Impulse. Then, having developed these three ways of relating to his house, the monkey begins to label and categorize it: "This is a window. This corner is pleasant. That wall frightens me and is bad." He develops a conceptual framework with which to label and categorize and evaluate his house, his world, according to whether he desires, hates, or feels indifferent to it. This is the Fourth Skandha, Concept.

The monkey's development through the Fourth Skandha has been fairly logical and predictable. But the pattern of development begins to break down as he enters the Fifth Skandha, Consciousness. The thought pattern becomes irregular and unpredictable and the monkey begins to hallucinate, to dream.

When we speak of "hallucination" or "dream," it means that we attach values to things and events which they do not necessarily have. We have definite opinions about the way things are and should be. This is projection: we project our version of things onto what is there. Thus we become completely immersed in a world of our own creation, a world of conflicting values and opinions. Hallucination, in this sense, is a misinterpretation of things and events, reading into the phenomenal world meanings which it does not have.

This is what the monkey begins to experience at the level of the Fifth Skandha. Having tried to get out and having failed, he feels dejected, helpless, and so he begins to go completely insane. Because he is so tired of struggling, it is very tempting for him to relax and let his mind wander and hallucinate. This is the creation of the Six *Lokas* or Six Realms. There is a great deal of discussion in the Buddhist tradition about hell beings, people in heaven, the human world, the animal realm, and other psychological states of being. These are the different kinds of projections, the dream worlds we create for ourselves.

Having struggled and failed to escape, having experienced claustrophobia and pain, this monkey begins to wish for something good, something beautiful and seductive. So the first realm he begins to hallucinate is the *Deva* Loka, the God Realm, "heaven," a place filled with beautiful, splendid things. The monkey dreams of strolling out of his house, walking in luxuriant fields, eating ripe fruit, sitting and swinging in the trees, living a life of freedom and ease.

Then he also begins to hallucinate the *Asura* Realm, or the Realm of the Jealous Gods. Having experienced the dream of heaven, the monkey wants to defend and maintain his great bliss and happiness. He suffers from paranoia, worrying that others may try to take his treasures from him, and so he begins to feel jealousy. He is proud of himself, has enjoyed his creation of the God Realm, and this has led him into jealousy of the Asura Realm.

Then he also perceives the earth-bound quality of these experiences. Instead of simply alternating between jealousy and pride, he begins to feel comfortable, at home in the "human world," the "earthy world." It is the world of just leading a regular life, doing things ordinarily, in a mundane fashion. This is the Human Realm.

But then the monkey also senses that something is a bit dull, something is not quite flowing. This is because, as he progresses from the Realm of the Gods to the Realm of the Jealous Gods to the Realm of Human Beings and his hallucinations become more and more solid, then this whole development begins to feel rather heavy and stupid. At this point he is born into the Animal Realm. He would rather crawl or moo or bark than enjoy the pleasure of pride or envy. This is the simplicity of the animals.

Then the process is intensified, and the monkey starts to experience a desperate feeling of starvation, because he really does not want to descend to any lower realms. He would like to return to the pleasure realms of the gods; so he begins to feel hunger and thirst, a tremendous feeling of nostalgia for what he remembers once having had. This is the Realm of the Hungry Ghosts or *Preta* Realm.

Then there is a sudden losing of faith and the monkey begins to doubt himself and his world, begins to react violently. All this is a terrible nightmare. He realizes that such a nightmare could not be true and he begins to hate himself for creating all this horror. This is the dream of the Hell Realm, the last of the Six Realms.

Throughout the entire development of the Six Realms the monkey has experienced discursive thoughts, ideas, fantasies, and whole thought patterns. Up to the level of the Fifth Skandha his process of psychological evolution has been very regular and predictable. From the First Skandha each successive development arose in a systematic pattern, like an overlay of tiles on a roof. But now the monkey's state of mind becomes very distorted and disturbed, as suddenly this mental jigsaw puzzle erupts and his thought patterns become irregular and unpredictable. This seems to be our state of mind as we come to the teachings and the practice of meditation. This is the place from which we must start our practice.

I think that it is very important to discuss the basis of the path—ego, our confusion—before we speak of liberation and freedom. If I were only to discuss the experience of liberation, that would be very dangerous. This is why we begin by considering the development of ego. It is a kind of psychological portrait of our mental states. I am afraid this has not been an especially beautiful talk, but we have to face the facts. That seems to be the process of working on the path.

Q: Could you say something more about what you mean by the "blackout?"

A: It is nothing particularly profound. It is just that at the level of the First Skandha we have worked very hard on trying to solidify space. We have worked so hard and with such speed that intelligence suddenly collapses. This could be said to be a kind of reverse satori, reverse enlightenment experience, the experience of ignorance. You suddenly go into a trance, because you have worked so hard. This is something which you have actually *achieved*, a masterpiece, all this solidity. And having achieved it completely, then suddenly you are overwhelmed by it. It is a meditation of its kind, a sort of reverse samadhi.

Q: Do you think that people have to be aware of death in order actually to be alive?
A: I don't think you have to be particularly aware of death, in the sense of analyzing it, but you just have to see what you are. Often we tend to look for the positive side, the beauty of spirituality, and ignore ourselves as we are. This is the greatest danger. If we are engaged in self-analysis, our spiritual practice is trying to find some ultimate analysis, an ultimate self-deception. Ego's intelligence is tremendously talented. It can distort anything. If one seizes on the ideas of spirituality or self-analysis or transcendence of ego, immediately ego takes hold of them and translates them into self-deception.

Q: When the monkey starts to hallucinate, is it something he has known before? Where does hallucination come from?
A: It is a kind of instinct, a secondary instinct, the ape instinct that we all have. If there is pain, then one will hallucinate pleasure, by contrast. There is the urge to defend oneself, establish one's territory.

Q: Equipped only with the level of consciousness we now have, are we not doomed to fight and struggle hopelessly at this level, unless we can get back to the space you have been describing?

A: Of course we are going to fight all the time, there is no end. We could go on talking forever about the succession of struggles we will endure. There is no other answer at all, except just as you said, trying to find the primordial space again. Otherwise we are stuck in the psychological attitude of *this* as opposed to *that*, which is an obstacle. We are always fighting an opponent. There is never a moment when we give up fighting. The problem is duality, warfare in terms of I and my opponent.

The practice of meditation is a completely different way of working. One has to change one's whole attitude and way of conducting life. One has to change all one's policies, so to speak. This could be very painful. Suddenly one begins to realize, "If I do not fight, how am I going to deal with my enemies? It is all very well for me not to fight, but what about them? They are still going to be there." That is the interesting point.

Q: To see the wall and recognize that you are there and not go further—it seems like a very dangerous position.
A: That is precisely it; it isn't dangerous. It might be painful at the time to realize that the wall is solid and that you are trapped inside it, but that is the interesting point.

Q: But weren't you just saying that it is instinctive to want to return to the other state, the open space?
A: Of course, but this monkey will not let himself just *be* anymore. He continually fights, or else he is involved in hallucinations. He never stops, never allows himself to actually feel anything properly. That is the problem. That is why simply stopping, just allowing a gap, is the first step in the practice of meditation.

Q: Say you have a barrier, an inhibition, and you are very aware of it. Should the inhibition just disappear through your awareness of it?

A: The whole point is that we must not attempt to figure out how we are going to escape our dilemma, but for now we must think about all these claustrophobic rooms that we are in. This is the first step to learning. We have to actually identify ourselves and feel ourselves properly. This will provide us with inspiration for further study. We had better not speak of getting free yet.

Q: Would you say that these claustrophobic rooms were intellectual fabrications?

A: The intensity of the primordial intelligence triggers us off all the time. All these activities of the monkey are, therefore, not to be regarded as something we should escape but as something which is a product of primordial intelligence. The more we try to struggle, the more we will discover that the walls really are solid. The more energy we put into struggle, by that much will we strengthen the walls, because the walls need our attention to solidify them. Whenever we pay more attention to the walls, we begin to feel the hopelessness of escape.

Q: What does the monkey perceive when he looks out of the five windows of the house?

A: Well, he perceives the east, west, south and north.

Q: How do they look to him?

A: A square world.

Q: What about outside the house?

A: Well, a square world, because he sees through windows.

Q: He doesn't see anything in the distance?
A: He could, but it is also a square picture, because it is like hanging a picture on the wall, isn't it?

Q: What happens to the monkey when he takes a little LSD or peyote?
A: He has already taken it.

The Six Realms

When we left the monkey, he was in the Hell Realm, trying to kick and claw and push his way through the walls of his house. The monkey's experiences in the Hell Realm are quite terrifying and horrific. He finds himself walking through gigantic fields of red-hot iron, or being chained and marked with black lines and cut apart, or roasting in hot iron cubicles, or boiling in large cauldrons. These and the other hallucinations of Hell are generated from an environment of claustrophobia and aggression. There is a feeling of being trapped in a small space with no air to breathe and no room in which to move about. Trapped as he is, the monkey not only tries to destroy the walls of his claustrophobic prison; he even attempts to kill himself in order to escape his excruciating and continuous pain. But he cannot really kill himself, and his suicide attempts only intensify his torture. The more the monkey struggles to destroy or control the walls, the more solid and oppressive they become, until at some point the intensity of the monkey's aggression wears out a bit and, instead of battling with the walls, he stops relating to them, stops communicating with them. He becomes paralyzed, frozen, remaining enveloped in pain without struggling to escape it. Here he experiences the various tortures involving freezing and dwelling in harsh, barren, desolate areas.

However, eventually the monkey begins to become exhausted from his struggle. The intensity of the Hell Realm begins to diminish, the monkey begins to relax, and suddenly he sees the possibility of a more open, spacious way to be. He hungers for this new state, and this is the Realm of the Hungry Ghost or Preta Loka: the feeling of impoverishment and hunger for relief. In the Hell Realm he had been too busy struggling to even have time to consider the possibility of relief. Now he experiences great hunger for more pleasurable, spacious conditions and fantasizes numerous ways to satisfy his hunger. He may imagine that he sees far away from him some open space, but when he approaches it, he finds a vast terrifying desert. Or he may see in the distance a huge fruit tree, but as he goes closer to it, he discovers that it is barren or that someone is guarding it. Or the monkey may fly to a seemingly lush and fertile valley, only to find it filled with poisonous insects and the repelling smells of rotting vegetation. In each of his fantasies he glimpses the possibility of satisfaction, reaches out for it, and is quickly disappointed. Each time he seems about to achieve pleasure, he is rudely awakened from his idyllic dream; but his hunger is so demanding that he is not daunted and so continues to constantly churn out fantasies of future satisfaction. The pain of disappointment involves the monkey in a love-hate relationship with his dreams. He is fascinated by them, but the disappointment is so painful that he is repelled by them as well.

The torture of the Hungry Ghost Realm is not so much the pain of not finding what he wants; rather it is the insatiable hunger itself which causes pain. Probably if the monkey found large quantities of food, he would not touch it at all; or else he would eat everything and then desire more. This is because, fundamentally, the monkey is fascinated with *being* hungry rather than with *satisfying* his hunger. The quick frustration of his attempts to satisfy his hunger enables him to be hungry again. So the pain and hunger of the Preta Loka, as with the aggression of the Hell Realm and the preoccupations of the other realms, provide the monkey with something exciting to occupy himself, something solid to relate to, something to make him feel secure that he exists as a real person. He is afraid to give up this security and entertainment, afraid to venture out into the unknown world of open space. He would rather stay in his familiar prison, no matter how painful and oppressive it might be.

However, as the monkey is repeatedly frustrated in his attempts to fulfill his fantasies, he begins to become somewhat resentful and at the same time resigned. He begins to give up the intensity of hunger and relax further into a set series of habitual responses to the world. He ignores other ways of dealing with life experiences, relies on the same set of responses, and in this way limits his world: a dog tries to smell everything with which it comes into contact; a cat takes no interest in television. This is the Animal Realm, the realm of stupidity. The monkey blinds himself to what is around him and refuses to explore new territory, clinging to familiar goals and familiar irritations. He is intoxicated with his safe, self-contained, familiar world and so fixes his attention on familiar goals and pursues them with unswerving and stubborn determination. Thus the Animal Realm is symbolized by the pig. A pig just eats whatever comes in front of its nose. It does not look right or left; it just goes right through, just does it. It does not matter to the pig if it has to swim through a tremendous mud pool or face other obstacles; it just plows through and eats whatever appears in front of it.

But eventually the monkey begins to realize that he can pick and choose his pleasures and pains. He begins to become somewhat more intelligent, discriminating between pleasurable and painful experiences in an effort to maximize pleasure and minimize pain. This is the Human Realm, the realm of discriminating passion. Here the monkey stops to consider what it is that he is reaching for. He becomes more discriminating, considers alternatives, thinks more, and therefore hopes and fears more. This is the Human Realm, the realm of passion and intellect. The monkey becomes more intelligent. He does not simply grasp; he explores, feels textures, compares things. If he decides that he wants something, he tries to grasp it, draw it to him and possess it. For example, if the monkey were to want a beautiful silk material, he would go to different shops and feel the texture of their materials to see if any one of them was exactly what he wanted. When he came to the material which precisely fit his preconception, or the nearest thing to it, he would feel it and say, "Ah, that's right. Isn't it beautiful? I think it's worth buying." Then he would pay for it and take it home and show it to his friends and ask them to feel it and appreciate the texture of his beautiful material. In the Human Realm the monkey is always thinking about how to possess pleasurable things: "Maybe I should buy a teddy bear to take to bed—something lovable, cuddly, soft, warm and hairy."

But the monkey discovers that, although he is intelligent and can manipulate his world to achieve some pleasure, still he cannot hold on to pleasure nor can he always get what he

wants. He is plagued by illness, old age, death—by frustra-
tions and problems of all kinds. Pain is the constant companion of his pleasures.

So he begins, quite logically, to deduce the possibility of
heaven, the complete elimination of pain and achievement of
pleasure. His version of heaven may be the acquisition of
extreme wealth or power or fame—whatever it is he would
like his world to be, and he becomes preoccupied with achievement and competition. This is the Asura Realm, the Realm
of the Jealous Gods. The monkey dreams of ideal states that
are superior to the pleasures and pains of the Human Realm
and is always trying to achieve these states, always trying to
be better than anyone else. In his constant struggle to achieve
perfection of some sort, the monkey becomes obsessed with
measuring his progress, with comparing himself to others.
Through developing increased control of his thoughts and
emotions and therefore greater concentration, he is able to
manipulate his world more successfully than in the Human
Realm. But his preoccupation with always being best, with
always being master of a situation, makes him insecure and
anxious. He must always struggle to control his territory,
overcoming all threats to his achievements. He is always fighting for mastery of his world.

The ambition to gain victory and the fear of losing a battle
provide a sense of being alive as well as cause irritation. The
monkey constantly loses sight of his ultimate goal, but is still
driven on by his ambition to be better. He is obsessed with
competition and achievement. He seeks out pleasurable, ap-
pealing situations that seem beyond his reach and tries to
draw them into his territory. When it is too difficult to achieve
his goals, he may shy away from the struggle and condemn
himself for not disciplining himself, for not working harder.

So the monkey is caught in a world of unfulfilled ideals, self-condemnation and fear of failure.

Eventually the monkey may achieve his goal—become a millionaire, leader of a country, famous artist. At first, upon achieving his goal, he will still feel somewhat insecure; but sooner or later he begins to realize that he has made it, that he is there, that he is in heaven. Then he begins to relax, to appreciate and dwell upon his achievements, shielding out undesirable things. It is an hypnotic-like state, natural concentration. This blissful and proud state is the Deva Loka or Realm of the Gods. Figuratively, the bodies of the gods are made out of light. They do not have to bother with earth-bound concerns. If they want to make love, just glancing and smiling at each other satisfies them. If they want to eat, they just direct their minds toward beautiful sights which feed them. It is the utopian world which human beings expect it to be. Everything happens easily, naturally, automatically. Whatever the monkey hears is musical, whatever he sees is colorful, whatever he feels is pleasant. He has achieved a kind of self-hypnosis, a natural state of concentration which blocks out of his mind everything he might find irritating or undesirable.

Then the monkey discovers that he can go beyond the sensual pleasures and beauties of the God Realm and enter into the *dhyana* or concentration states of the Realm of the Formless Gods, which is the ultimate refinement of the Six Realms. He realizes that he can achieve purely mental pleasure, the most subtle and durable of all, that he is able to maintain his sense of a solid self continuously by expanding the walls of his prison to seemingly include the whole cosmos, thereby conquering change and death. First he dwells upon the idea of limitless space. He watches limitless space; he is

here and limitless space is there and he watches it. He im-
poses his preconception on the world, creates limitless space,
and feeds himself with this experience. Then the next stage
is concentration upon the idea of limitless consciousness. Here
one does not dwell on limitless space alone, but one also dwells
upon the intelligence which perceives that limitless space as
well. So ego watches limitless space and consciousness from
its central headquarters. The empire of ego is completely
extended, even the central authority cannot imagine how far
its territory extends. Ego becomes a huge, gigantic beast.

Ego has extended itself so far that it begins to lose track
of the boundary of its territory. Wherever it tries to define
its boundary, it seems to exclude part of its territory. Finally,
it concludes that there is no way of defining its boundaries.
The size of its empire cannot be conceived or imagined. Since
it includes everything, it cannot be defined as this or that.
So the ego dwells on the idea of not this and not that, the idea
that it cannot conceive or imagine itself. But finally even this
state of mind is surpassed when the ego realizes that the idea
that it is inconceivable and unimaginable is in itself a con-
ception. So the ego dwells on the idea of *not* not this, and *not*
not that. This idea of the impossibility of asserting anything is
something which ego feeds on, takes pride in, identifies with
and therefore uses to maintain its continuity. This is the
highest level of concentration and achievement that confused,
samsaric mind can attain.

The monkey has managed to reach the ultimate level of
achievement; but he has not transcended the dualistic logic
upon which achievement depends. The walls of the monkey's
house are still solid, still have the quality of "other" in a
subtle sense. The monkey may have achieved a temporary
harmony and peace and bliss through a seeming union with

his projections; but the whole thing is subtly fixed, a closed world. He has become as solid as the walls, has achieved the state of Egohood. He is still preoccupied with securing and enhancing himself, still caught up in fixed ideas and concepts about the world and himself, still taking the fantasies of the fifth skandha seriously. Since his state of consciousness is based on concentration, on dwelling upon other, he must continually check and maintain his achievement. "What a relief to be here in the Realm of the Gods. I finally made it. I have really got it now. But wait a minute . . . Have I really made it? Ah, there it is. Yes, I've made it. *I* have made it." The monkey thinks that he has achieved nirvana, but actually he has achieved only a temporary state of Egohood.

Sooner or later the absorption wears out and the monkey begins to panic. He feels threatened, confused, vulnerable and plunges into the Realm of the Jealous Gods. But the anxiety and envy of the Realm of the Jealous Gods is overpowering and the monkey becomes preoccupied with figuring out what has gone wrong. So he returns to the Human Realm. But the Human Realm is very painful as well: the continual effort to figure out what is happening, what has gone wrong, just increases the pain and confusion. So the monkey escapes the hesitation and critical perspective of the human intellect and plunges into the animal realm where he just plods along, ignoring what is around him, playing deaf and dumb to messages that might challenge the security of following narrow, familiar ways. But messages from the environment break through and a hunger for something more develops. Nostalgia for the God Realm becomes very strong and the intensity of the struggle to go back to it increases. The monkey fantasizes enjoying the pleasures of the God Realm. But the satisfaction derived from the fantasy of fulfilling his hunger is brief and he quickly finds himself hungry again. The hunger goes on and on, until finally he is overwhelmed by the frustration of his recurring hunger and plunges into a still more intense struggle to fulfill his desires. The monkey's aggression is so intense that the environment around him responds with equal aggression and an atmosphere of heat and claustrophobia develops. The monkey finds himself back in Hell. He has managed to make a full circle from hell to heaven and back again. This perpetual cycle of struggle, achievement, disillusionment and pain is the circle of samsara, the karmic chain reaction of dualistic fixation.

How can the monkey get out of this seemingly endless, self-contained cycle of imprisonment? It is in the Human Realm that the possibility of breaking the karmic chain or the circle of samsara, arises. The intellect of the Human Realm and the possibility of discriminating action allows room to question the whole process of struggle. There is a possibility for the monkey to question the obsession of relating to something, of getting something, to question the solidity of the worlds that he experiences. To do this, the monkey needs to develop panoramic awareness and transcendental knowledge. Panoramic awareness allows the monkey to see the space in which the struggle occurs so that he can begin to see its ironical and humorous quality. Instead of simply struggling, he begins to experience the struggle and see its futility. He laughs through the hallucinations. He discovers that when he does not fight the walls, they are not repulsive and hard but are actually warm, soft and penetrable. He finds that he does not have to leap from the five windows or break down the walls or even dwell upon them; he can step through them anywhere. That is why compassion or *karuna* is described as "soft and noble heart." It is a communication process that is soft, open and warm.

The clarity and precision of transcendental knowledge allows the monkey to see the walls in a different way. He begins to realize that the world was never outside of himself, that it was his own dualistic attitude, the separation of "I" and "other," that created the problem. He begins to understand that he himself is making the walls solid, that he is imprisoning himself through his ambition. And so he begins to realize that to be free of his prison he must give up his ambition to escape and accept the walls as they are.

Q: What if you never really felt that you had to struggle— you have never reached the point of wanting to get out of the house? Perhaps you are a bit afraid of what is outside the walls, so you use them as protection.
A: Somehow, if you are able to establish friendly terms with the walls, then there are no more walls, as such. Much as you would like to have the walls for protection, the walls will not be there anymore. It is very paradoxical that, the more you dislike the wall, the stronger and thicker the wall becomes, and the more you make friends with the wall, the more the wall disappears.

Q: I wonder if pain and pleasure are on the same footing as this intellectual discrimination between good and bad or right and wrong. Is this discrimination due to a subjective attitude?
A: I think pleasure and pain are born in the same kind of background. Generally people regard pain as bad and pleasure as good, so much so that pleasure is regarded as joy and

spiritual bliss, and is connected with heaven, while pain is associated with hell. So if one is able to see the absurdity and irony of trying to achieve pleasure by rejecting pain, fearing extreme pain and so striving toward pleasure, it is all very funny. There is some lacking of a sense of humor in people's attitudes toward pleasure and pain.

Q: You stated earlier that we hallucinate the phenomenal world and want to break out of it. I understand the Buddhist teaching to say that the phenomenal world is simply the manifestation of emptiness, so what would there be to break out of?
A: The point is that in the perception of ego the phenomenal world is very real, overwhelming, solid. It may in fact be hallucinatory, but as far as the monkey is concerned the hallucination is quite real and solid. From his confused point of view even thought becomes very solid and tangible. It is not good enough to say that these hallucinations do not exist because form is emptiness and emptiness is form. Try telling that to a neurotic monkey. As far as he is concerned, form exists as solid and heavy form. It is real to him because he is so obsessed with it that he does not allow any space to see otherwise. He is too busy continuously trying to reinforce his own existence. He never allows a gap. Thus there is no room for inspiration, no room to see other aspects, different angles of the situation. From the monkey's point of view the confusion is *real*. When you have a nightmare, at that moment it is real, terribly frightening. On the other hand, when you look back at the experience, it seems merely to have been a dream. You cannot use two different kinds of logic simultaneously. You have to see the confused aspect completely in order to see through it, to see the absurdity of it.

The Four Noble Truths

Having painted a colorful picture of the monkey with his many qualities—inquisitive, passionate, aggressive, and so on—we could at this point examine the details of how he might deal with his predicament.

One comes to an understanding and transcendence of ego by using meditation to work backwards through the Five Skandhas. And the last development of the Fifth Skandha is the neurotic and irregular thought patterns which constantly flit across the mind. Many different kinds of thoughts develop along with the monkey's hallucinating of the Six Realms: discursive thoughts, grasshopper-like thoughts, display-like thoughts, filmshow-like thoughts, etc. It is from this point of confusion that we must start; and in order to clarify the confusion it would be helpful to examine the ideas of the Four Noble Truths which constitute the first turning of the "Wheel of Dharma" by the Buddha.

The Four Noble Truths are: the truth of suffering, the truth of the origin of suffering, the truth of the goal, and the truth of the path. We start with the truth of suffering, which means that we must begin with the monkey's confusion and insanity.

We must begin to see the actuality of *duhkha*, a Sanskrit

word which means "suffering," "dissatisfaction," or "pain." Dissatisfaction occurs because the mind spins around in such a way that there seems to be no beginning and no end to its motion. Thought processes continue on and on: thoughts of the past, thoughts of the future, thoughts of the present moment. This creates irritation. Thoughts are prompted by and are also identical with dissatisfaction, duhkha, the constantly repeated feeling that something is lacking, incomplete in our lives. Somehow, something is not quite right, not quite enough. So we are always trying to fill the gap, to make things right, to find that extra bit of pleasure or security. The continuing action of struggle and preoccupation is very irritating and painful. Eventually, one begins to become irritated by just being "me."

So to understand the truth of duhkha is actually to understand mind's neurosis. We are driven here and there with so much energy. Whether we eat, sleep, work, play, whatever we do, life contains duhkha, dissatisfaction, pain. If we enjoy pleasure, we are afraid to lose it; we strive for more and more pleasure or try to contain it. If we suffer in pain, we want to escape it. We experience dissatisfaction all the time. All activities contain dissatisfaction or pain, continuously.

Somehow we pattern life in a way that never allows us enough time to actually taste its flavor. There is continual busyness, continual searching for the next moment, a continual grasping quality to life. That is duhkha, the First Noble Truth. Understanding and confronting suffering is the first step.

Having become acutely aware of our dissatisfaction, we begin to search for a reason for it, for the source of the dissatisfaction. By examining our thoughts and actions we discover that we are continually struggling to maintain and enhance ourselves. We realize that this struggle is the root of suffering. So we seek an understanding of the process of struggle: that is, of how ego develops and operates. This is the Second Noble Truth, the truth of the origin of suffering.

As we discussed in the chapters dealing with spiritual materialism, many people make the mistake of thinking that, since ego is the root of suffering, the goal of spirituality must be to conquer and destroy ego. They struggle to eliminate ego's heavy hand but, as we discovered earlier, that struggle is merely another expression of ego. We go around and around, trying to improve ourselves through struggle, until we realize that the ambition to improve ourselves is itself the problem. Insights come only when there are gaps in our struggle, only when we stop trying to rid ourselves of thought, when we cease siding with pious, good thoughts against bad, impure thoughts, only when we allow ourselves simply to see the nature of thought.

We begin to realize that there is a sane, awake quality within us. In fact this quality manifests itself only in the absence of struggle. So we discover the Third Noble Truth, the truth of the goal: that is, non-striving. We need only drop the effort to secure and solidify ourselves and the awakened state is present. But we soon realize that just "letting go" is only possible for short periods. We need some discipline to bring us to "letting be." We must walk a spiritual path. Ego must wear itself out like an old shoe, journeying from suffering to liberation.

So let us examine the spiritual path, the practice of meditation, the Fourth Noble Truth. Meditation practice is not an attempt to enter into a trance-like state of mind nor is it an attempt to become preoccupied with a particular object. There has developed, both in India and Tibet, a so-called system of meditation which might be called "concentration." That is to say that this practice of meditation is based on focusing the mind on a particular point so as to be better able to control the mind and concentrate. In such practice the student chooses an object to look at, think about, or visualize and then focuses his entire attention upon it. In so doing, he tends to develop by force a certain kind of mental calm. I call this kind of practice "mental gymnastics" because it does not attempt to deal with the totality of any given life-situation. It is based entirely on *this* or *that*, subject and object, rather than transcending the dualistic view of life.

The practice of samadhi on the other hand does not involve concentration. This is very important to realize. Concentration practices are largely ego-reinforcing, although not purposely intended as such. Still, concentration is practiced with a particular aim and object in mind, so we tend to become centralized in the "heart." We set out to concentrate upon a flower, stone or flame, and we gaze fixedly at the object, but mentally we are going into the heart as much as possible. We are trying to intensify the solid aspect of form, the qualities of stability and stillness. In the long run such a practice could be dangerous. Depending upon the intensity of the meditator's will-power, we might become introverted in a way which is too solemn, fixed and rigid. This sort of practice is not conducive to openness and energy nor to a sense of humor. It is too heavy and could easily become dogmatic, in the sense that those who become involved in such practices think in terms of imposing discipline upon themselves. We think it necessary to be very serious and solemn. This produces a competitive attitude in our thinking—the more we can render our minds captive, the more successful we are—which is a rather dogmatic, authoritarian approach. This way of thinking, always focused on the future, is habitual with ego: "I would like to see such and such results. I have an idealized theory or dream which I would like to put into effect." We tend to live in the future, our view of life colored by the expectation of achieving an ideal goal. Because of this expectation we miss the precision and openness and intelligence of the present. We are fascinated, blinded and overwhelmed by the idealized goal.

The competitive quality of ego can readily be seen in the materialistic world in which we live. If you want to become a millionaire, you first try to become a millionaire *psychologically*. You start by having an image of yourself as a millionaire and then work very hard towards that goal. You push yourself in that direction, regardless of whether or not you are able to achieve it. This approach creates a kind of blindfold, rendering you insensitive to the present moment because you are living too much in the future. One could take the same mistaken approach to the practice of meditation.

Inasmuch as real meditation practice is a way to step out of ego, the first point is not to focus yourself too much upon the future attainment of the awakened state of mind. The whole practice of meditation is essentially based upon the situation of this present moment, here and now, and means working with this situation, this present state of mind. Any meditation practice concerned with transcending ego is focused in the present moment. For this reason it is a very effective way to live. If you are completely aware of your present state of being and the situation around you, you cannot miss a thing. We may use various meditation techniques to facilitate this kind of awareness, but these techniques are simply a way of stepping out of ego. Technique is like a toy given to a child. When the child grows up, the toy is discarded. In the meantime technique is necessary in order to develop patience and to refrain from dreaming about the "spiritual experience." One's whole practice should be based on the relationship between you and nowness.

You do not have to push yourself into the practice of meditation but just let be. If you practice in this way, a feeling of space and ventilation automatically comes, the expression of the Buddha-nature or basic intelligence that is working its way through confusion. Then you begin to find the understanding of the "truth of the path," the Fourth Noble Truth, simplicity, such as the awareness of walking. First you become aware of standing, then you are aware that your right leg is lifting, swinging, touching, pressing; then the left leg is lifting, swinging, touching, pressing. There are many, many details of action involved in the simplicity and sharpness of being in this very moment, here, now.

And it is the same with the practice of the awareness of breathing. You become aware of the breath coming into your nostrils, going out and finally dissolving into the atmosphere. It is a very gradual and detailed process and acute precision is involved with its simplicity. If an act is simple, then you begin to realize its precision. One begins to realize that whatever we do in everyday life is beautiful and meaningful.

If you pour a cup of tea, you are aware of extending your arm and touching your hand to the teapot, lifting it and pouring the water. Finally the water touches your teacup and fills it, and you stop pouring and put the teapot down precisely, as in the Japanese tea ceremony. You become aware that each precise movement has dignity. We have long forgotten that activities can be simple and precise. Every act of our lives can contain simplicity and precision and can thus have tremendous beauty and dignity.

The process of communication can be beautiful, if we see it in terms of simplicity and precision. Every pause made in the process of speaking becomes a kind of punctuation. Speak, allow space, speak, allow space. It does not have to be a formal and solemn occasion necessarily, but it is beautiful that you are not rushing, that you are not talking at tremendous speed, raucously. We do not have to churn out information and then stop suddenly with a feeling of let-down in order to get a response from the other person. We could do things in a dignified and proper way. Just allow space. Space is as important in communicating to another person as talking. You do not have to overload the other person with words and ideas and smiles all at once. You can allow space, smile, say something, and then allow a gap, and then talk, and then space, punctuation. Imagine if we wrote letters without any punctuation. The communication would be very chaotic. You do not have to be self-conscious and rigid about allowing space; just feel the natural flow of it.

This practice of seeing the precision of situations at every moment, through such methods as the awareness of walking, is called *shamatha* (Pali: *samatha*) meditation. Shamatha meditation is associated with the Hinayana Path or the "lesser vehicle," the disciplined or narrow path. Shamatha means "peacefulness." There is a story concerning the Buddha which relates how he taught a village woman to develop such mindfulness in the act of drawing water from a well. He taught her to be aware of the precise movement of her hands and arms as she drew up the water. Such practice is the attempt to see the nowness quality in action, which is why it is known as "shamatha," the development of peace. When you see the nowness of the very moment, there is no room for anything but openness and peace.

Q: Could you say something more about allowing gaps to appear? I understand what you mean, but I do not understand how they come about, how someone allows a gap. How does one "let be?"

A: Actually this question leads into the next topic, the discussion of the Bodhisattva Path, the Mahayana Path of compassion and freedom, the wide path. However, to answer the question from the Hinayana point of view of simplicity, one should be completely satisfied with whatever situation arises and not look for entertainment from an external source. Generally, when we speak, we do not simply want to communicate to the other person, but we want a response as well. We want to be fed by the other person, which is a very egocentric way of communicating. We have to give up this desire to be fed, and then the gap automatically comes. We cannot produce the gap through effort.

Q: You said we have to prepare ourselves to enter the path. We cannot rush into it. We have to pause. Could you speak a bit more about this preparation?

A: In the beginning we have the feeling that the spiritual search is something very beautiful, something that will answer all our questions. We must go beyond this kind of hope and expectation. We might expect our teacher to solve all our problems, relieve all our doubts. But when we confront our teacher, he does not actually answer every question. He leaves many things for us to work out ourselves, which is a tremendous letdown and disappointment for us.

We have many expectations, especially if we seek a spiritual path and involve ourselves with spiritual materialism. We have the expectation that spirituality will bring us happiness and comfort, wisdom and salvation. This literal, egocentric way of regarding spirituality must be turned completely upside down. Finally, if we give up all hope of attaining any sort of enlightenment, then at that moment the path begins to open. It is like the situation of waiting for someone to arrive. You are about to give up all hope that he will ever come, you have begun to think that the notion of his arrival was simply a fantasy on your part, that he was never coming in the first place. The moment you give up hope, the person turns up. The spiritual path works in this way. It is a matter of wearing out all expectation. Patience is necessary. You do not have to push yourself too energetically into the path but just wait, just allow some space, do not be too busy trying to understand "reality." It is necessary first to see the motivation for our spiritual search. Ambition is unnecessary if we are going to start our path open-mindedly, with a mind that transcends both "good" and "bad."

A tremendous hunger for knowledge develops when we begin to realize the origin of duhkha. There will be a tremendous push to get beyond it. If we push ourselves too much, then the path of spirituality becomes instead the path of pain, confusion, and samsara, because we are very busy trying to save ourselves. We are too keen to learn something, too busy attending to our ambition to progress on the path rather than letting ourselves be and examining the whole process before we start. It is necessary not to rush onto the spiritual path but to prepare ourselves properly and thoroughly. Just wait. Wait and examine the whole process of the "spiritual search." Allow some gap.

The main point is that we have this basic intelligence that shines through our confusion. Consider the original analogy of the monkey. He wanted to get out of his house and so became very busy trying to escape, examining the walls and windows, climbing up and down. The tremendous energy that drives the monkey is the primeval intelligence which pushes us outward. This intelligence is not like a seed which you must nurture. It is like the sun that shines through gaps in the clouds. When we allow a gap, then spontaneous, intuitive understanding of how to proceed on the path suddenly, automatically comes to us. This was the experience of the Buddha. After he had studied numerous yogic disciplines under many Hindu masters, he realized that he could not achieve a completely awakened state simply by trying to apply these techniques. So he stopped and decided to work on himself as he already was. That is the basic instinct which is pushing its way through. It is very necessary to acknowledge this basic instinct. It tells us that we are not condemned people, that we are not fundamentally bad or lacking.

Q: How does one deal with practical life situations while trying to be simple and experience space?
A: You see, in order to experience open space one also must experience the solidity of earth, of form. They are interdependent. Often we romanticize open space and then we fall into traps. As long as we do not romanticize open space as a wondrous place but rather relate that space to earth, then we will avoid these traps. Space cannot be experienced without the outline of the earth to define it. If we are going to paint a picture of open space, we must express it in terms of the earth's horizon. So it is necessary to bring oneself back to the problems of everyday life, the kitchen-sink problems. That is why the simplicity and precision of everyday activitives is very important. If you perceive open space, you should bring yourself back to your old, familiar, claustrophobic life-situations and look into them more closely, examine them, absorb

yourself into them, until the absurdity of their solidity strikes you and you can see their spaciousness as well.

Q: How does one relate to the impatience that accompanies the waiting period?

A: Impatience means that you do not have a complete understanding of the process. If you see the completeness of each action, then you will not be impatient any more.

Q: I experience calm thoughts as well as neurotic thoughts. Are these calm thoughts something I should cultivate?

A: In the practice of meditation all thoughts are the same: pious thoughts, very beautiful thoughts, religious thoughts, calm thoughts—they are all still thoughts. You do not try to cultivate calm thoughts and suppress so-called neurotic thoughts. This is an interesting point. When we speak of treading the path of the dharma, which is the Fourth Noble Truth, it does not mean that we become religious, calm, good. Trying to be calm, trying to be good, is also an aspect of striving, of neuroticism. Religiously inclined thoughts are the watcher, the judge, and confused, worldly thoughts are the actor, the doer. For instance if you meditate, you might experience ordinary domestic thoughts and at the same time there is a watcher saying, "You shouldn't do this, you shouldn't do that, but you should come back to meditation." These pious thoughts are still thoughts and should not be cultivated.

Q: Could you say something more about using pauses as well as speech to communicate, and how this process relates to ego?

A: Usually, when we communicate with another person, we are driven by a kind of neurotic speed. We must begin to allow some spontaneity to penetrate this speed so that we do not push ourselves onto the person with whom we are communicating, do not impose ourselves, do not overload the other person. In particular, when we speak of something in which we are very interested, we do not just talk but we leap at the other person. Spontaneity is always there, but it is clouded over by thought. Whenever there is a gap in the cloudbank of thought, it shines through. Reach out and acknowledge that first openness and through that opening the basic intelligence will begin to function.

Q: Many people are aware of the truth of suffering but do not move on to the second step, awareness of the origin of suffering. Why is that?

A: I think that it is largely a matter of paranoia. We want to escape. We want to run away from pain rather than regard it as a source of inspiration. We feel the suffering to be bad enough, so why investigate it further? Some people who suffer a great deal and realize that they cannot escape their suffering really begin to understand it. But most people are too busy attempting to rid themselves of irritation, too busy seeking distractions from themselves to look into the material they already have. It is too embarrassing to look into it. This is the attitude of paranoia: if you look too closely, you will find something fearful. But in order to be a completely inspired person like Gautama Buddha, you have to be very open-minded and intelligent, an inquisitive person. You have to want to explore everything, even though it may be ugly, painful or repulsive. This kind of scientific-mindedness is very important.

Q: In the awakened mind, where does motivation come in?

A: Inspired motivation comes from something beyond ¦ thought, something beyond the conceptualized ideas of "good" and "bad," "desirable" and "undesirable." Beyond thought there is a kind of intelligence which is our basic nature, our background, an intuitive primordial intelligence, a feeling of space, a creative open way of dealing with situations. This kind of motivation is not intellectual: it is intuitive, precise.

Q: Can one work on one's mind by controlling the physical situation?

A: Whatever you do with the situations of life, there is always a communication going on between mind and matter. But one cannot rely upon the gadgetry of matter alone; you cannot get around the problems of mind by manipulating things external to it. We see so many people in our society trying to do just this. People put on robes and renounce the world and lead very austere lives, renouncing every common habit of human behavior. But eventually they will have to deal with their confused minds. Confusion originates in mind, so one has to start directly with mind rather than attempting to go around it. If one is trying to get around mental confusion by manipulating the physical world, then I do not think it will work.

In the dance of life, matter reflects mind and mind reacts to matter. There is a continual exchange. If one is holding a lump of rock, one should feel the solid earth qualities of rock. One has to learn how to communicate with the rocklike quality. If one is holding a flower, then the particular shape and color of the petals connect to our psychology as well. We cannot completely ignore the symbolism of the external world.

However, in the beginning as we attempt to confront our own neuroses, we must be very direct and not think that we can evade the problems of mind by playing with matter. For instance, if a person is psychologically unbalanced, completely confused, like the monkey we have been discussing, and if we dress him in the robes of the Buddha or sit him in a meditation posture, his mind will still spin around in the same way. But later on, when he learns to settle himself down and becomes a simple monkey, then there might be a certain effectiveness in taking him into a quiet place or retreat.

Q: When I see the ugliness in myself, I do not know how to accept it. I try to avoid it or change it rather than accept it.

A: Well, you do not have to hide it. You do not have to change it. Investigate it further. When you see the ugliness in yourself, that is just a preconception. You see it as ugliness, which is still connected with the ideas of "good" and "bad." But you have to transcend even those words, "good" and "bad." You have to get beyond words and conceptualized ideas and just get into what you are, deeper and deeper. The first glimpse is not quite enough: you have to examine the details without judging, without using words and concepts. Opening to oneself fully is opening to the world.

The Bodhisattva Path

We have discussed the Hinayana meditation practice of simplicity and precision. By allowing a gap, space in which things may be as they are, we begin to appreciate the clear simplicity and precision of our lives. This is the beginning of meditation practice. We begin to penetrate the Fifth Skanda, cutting through the busyness and speed of discursive thought, the cloud of "gossip" that fills our minds. The next step is to work with emotions.

Discursive thought might be compared to the blood circulation which constantly feeds the muscles of our system, the emotions. Thoughts link and sustain the emotions so that, as we go about our daily lives, we experience an ongoing flow of mental gossip punctuated by more colorful and intense bursts of emotion. The thoughts and emotions express our basic attitudes toward and ways of relating to the world and form an environment, a fantasy realm in which we live. These "environments" are the Six Realms, and although one particular realm may typify the psychology of a particular individual, still that person will constantly experience the emotions connected with the other realms as well.

In order to work with these realms we must begin to view situations in a more panoramic way, which is *vipashyana*

(Pali: *vipassana*) meditation. We must become aware not only of the precise details of an activity, but also of the situation as a whole. Vipashyana involves awareness of space, the atmosphere in which precision occurs. If we see the precise details of our activity, this awareness also creates a certain space. Being aware of a situation on a small scale also brings awareness on a larger scale. Out of this develops panoramic awareness, *mahavipashyana* (Pali: *mahavipassana*) meditation: that is, awareness of the overall pattern rather than the focusing of attention upon details. We begin to see the pattern of our fantasies rather than being immersed in them. We discover that we need not struggle with our projections, that the wall that separates us from them is our own creation. The insight into the insubstantial nature of ego is prajna, transcendental knowledge. As we glimpse prajna we relax, realizing that we no longer have to maintain the existence of ego. We can afford to be open and generous. Seeing another way of dealing with our projections brings intense joy. This is the first spiritual level of attainment of the bodhisattva, the first *bhumi*. We enter the Bodhisattva Path, the Mahayana Path, the open way, the path of warmth and openness.

In mahavipashyana meditation there is a vast expanse of space between us and objects. We are aware of the space between the situation and ourselves and anything can happen in that space. Nothing is happening here or there in terms of relationship or battle. In other words, we are not imposing our conceptualized ideas, names and categories on experience, but we feel the openness of space in every situation. In this way awareness becomes very precise and all-encompassing.

Mahavipashyana meditation means allowing things to be as they are. We begin to realize that this needs no effort on our part because things *are* as they are. We do not have to look at them in that way: they *are* that way. And so we begin to really appreciate openness and space, that we have space in which to move about, that we do not have to try to be aware because we already are aware. So the Mahayana Path is the open way, the wide path. It involves the open-minded willingness to allow oneself to be awake, to allow one's instinct to spring out.

Previously we discussed allowing space in order to communicate, but that kind of practice is very deliberate and self-conscious. When we practice mahavipashyana meditation, we do not simply watch ourselves communicate, deliberately allowing a gap, deliberately waiting; but we communicate and then just space out, so to speak. Let be and not care anymore; don't possess the letting be as belonging to you, as your creation. Open, let be and *disown*. Then the spontaneity of the awakened state springs out.

The Mahayana scriptures speak of those who are completely ready to open, those who are just about ready to open and those who have the potential to open. Those who have the potential are intellectual people who are interested in the subject but who do not allow enough room for this instinct to spring out. Those who are almost ready are quite open-minded, but they are watching themselves more than necessary. Those who are completely ready to open have heard the secret word, the password of *tathagata*: someone has already done it, somebody has already crossed over, it is the open path, it is possible, it is the tathagata path. Therefore, disregarding how or when or why, simply open. It is a beautiful thing, it has already happened to someone else, why not to you? Why do you discriminate between "me" and the rest of the tathagatas?

"Tathagata" means "those who have experienced the *tatha-*

ta," which is, "as it is": those who have experienced "as it is."
In other words, the idea of tathagata is a way of inspiration,
a starting point; it tells us that other people have already made
it, that others have already experienced it. This instinct has
already inspired someone, the instinct of "awake," of openness, of coolness in the sense of intelligence.

The path of the bodhisattva is for those who are brave and
convinced of the powerful reality of the tathagata-nature
which exists within themselves. Those actually awakened by
such an idea as "tathagata" are on the Bodhisattva Path, the
path of the brave warrior who trusts in his potential to complete the journey, who trusts in the Buddha-nature. The word
"bodhisattva" means: "he who is brave enough to walk on
the path of the bodhi." "Bodhi" means "awake," "the
awakened state." This is not to say that the bodhisattva must
already be fully awake; but he is willing to walk the path of
the awakened ones.

This path consists of six transcendental activities which take
place spontaneously. They are: transcendental generosity, discipline, patience, energy, meditation and knowledge. These
virtues are called "the six *paramitas*," because "param"
means "other side" or "shore," "other side of the river," and
"ita" means "arrived." "Paramita" means "arriving at the
other side or shore," which indicates that the activities of the
bodhisattva must have the vision, the understanding which
transcends the centralized notions of ego. The bodhisattva is
not trying to be good or kind, but he is spontaneously compassionate.

Generosity

Transcendental generosity is generally misunderstood in the
study of the Buddhist scriptures as meaning being kind to

someone who is lower than you. Someone has this pain and suffering and you are in a superior position and can save them—which is a very simple-minded way of looking down upon someone. But in the case of the bodhisattva, generosity is not so callous. It is something very strong and powerful; it is communication.

Communication must transcend irritation, otherwise it will be like trying to make a comfortable bed in a briar patch. The penetrating qualities of external color, energy, and light will come toward us, penetrating our attempts to communicate like a thorn pricking our skin. We will wish to subdue this intense irritation and our communication will be blocked.

Communication must be radiation and receiving and exchange. Whenever irritation is involved, then we are not able to see properly and fully and clearly the spacious quality of that which is coming toward us, that which is presenting itself as communication. The external world is immediately rejected by our irritation which says, "No, no, this irritates me, go away." Such an attitude is the complete opposite of transcendental generosity.

So the bodhisattva must experience the complete communication of generosity, transcending irritation and self-defensiveness. Otherwise, when thorns threaten to prick us, we feel that we are being attacked, that we must defend ourselves. We run away from the tremendous opportunity for communication that has been given to us, and we have not been brave enough even to look to the other shore of the river. We are looking back and trying to run away.

Generosity is a willingness to give, to open without philosophical or pious or religious motives, just simply doing what is required at any moment in any situation, not being afraid to receive anything. Opening could take place in the middle of a highway. We are not afraid that smog and dust or people's hatreds and passions will overwhelm us; we simply open, completely surrender, give. This means that we do not judge, do not evaluate. If we attempt to judge or evaluate our experience, if we try to decide to what extent we should open, to what extent we should remain closed, then openness will have no meaning at all and the idea of paramita, of transcendental generosity, will be in vain. Our action will not transcend anything, will cease to be the act of a bodhisattva.

The whole implication of the idea of transcendence is that we see through the limited notions, the limited conceptions, the warfare mentality of *this* as opposed to *that*. Generally, when we look at an object, we do not allow ourselves to see it properly. Automatically we see our version of the object instead of actually seeing that object as it is. Then we are quite satisfied, because we have manufactured our own version of the thing within ourselves. Then we comment on it, we judge, we take or reject; but there is no real communication going on at all.

So transcendental generosity is giving whatever you have. Your action must be completely open, completely naked. It is not for you to make judgments; it is for the recipients to make the gesture of receiving. If the recipients are not ready for your generosity, they will not receive it. If they are ready for it, they will come and take it. This is the selfless action of the bodhisattva. He is not self-conscious: "Am I making any mistakes?"; "Am I being careful?"; "To whom should I open?" He never takes sides. The bodhisattva will, figuratively just lie like a corpse. Let people look at you and examine you. You are at their disposal. Such noble action, such complete action, action that does not contain any hypocrisy,

any philosophical or religious judgment at all. That is why it
is transcendental. That is why it is paramita. It is beautiful.

Discipline

And if we proceed further and examine the paramita of "morality" or "discipline," the *shila* paramita, we find that the
same principles apply. That is, shila or discipline is not a
matter of binding oneself to a fixed set of laws or patterns. For
if a bodhisattva is completely selfless, a completely open person, then he will act according to openness, will not have to
follow rules; he will simply fall into patterns. It is impossible
for the bodhisattva to destroy or harm other people, because
he embodies transcendental generosity. He has opened himself
completely and so does not discriminate between *this* and *that*.
He just acts in accordance with what *is*. From another person's
point of view—if someone were observing the bodhisattva—
he always appears to act correctly, always seems to do the
right thing at the right time. But if we were to try to imitate
him, it would be impossible to do so, because his mind is so
precise, so accurate that he never makes mistakes. He never
runs into unexpected problems, never creates chaos in a destructive way. He just falls into patterns. Even if life seems
to be chaotic, he just falls in, participates in the chaos and
somehow things sort themselves out. The bodhisattva is able
to cross the river so to speak, without falling into its turbu-
lence.

If we are completely open, not watching ourselves at all,
but being completely open and communicating with situations
as they are, then action is pure, absolute, superior. However,
if we attempt to achieve pure conduct through effort, our action will be clumsy. However pure it may be, still there will

be clumsiness and rigidity involved. In the case of the bodhi-sattva his whole action is flowing, there is no rigidity at all. Everything just fits into place, as if someone had taken years and years to figure out the whole situation. The bodhisattva does not act in a premeditated way; he just communicates. He starts from the generosity of openness and falls into the pat-tern of the situation. It is an often-used metaphor that the bodhisattva's conduct is like the walk of an elephant. Ele-phants do not hurry; they just walk slowly and surely through the jungle, one step after another. They just sail right along. They never fall nor do they make mistakes. Each step they take is solid and definite.

Patience

The next act of the bodhisattva is patience. Actually you can-not really divide the six activities of the bodhisattva into strictly separate practices. One leads into and embodies the next. So in the case of the paramita of patience, this action is not a matter of trying to control oneself, trying to become a hard worker, trying to be an extremely forebearing person, disregarding one's physical or mental weakness, going on and on and on until one completely drops dead. But patience also involves skillful means, as with discipline and generosity.

Transcendental patience never expects anything. Not ex-pecting anything, we do not get impatient. However, generally in our lives we expect a lot, we push ourselves, and this kind of action is very much based on impulse. We find something exciting and beautiful and we push ourselves very hard towards it, and sooner or later we are pushed back. The more we push forward, the more we will be pushed back, because impulse is such a strong driving force without wisdom. The action of impulse is like that of a person running without eyes to see, like that of a blind man trying to reach his destination. But the action of the bodhisattva never provokes a reaction. The bodhisattva can accommodate himself to any situation because he never desires or is fascinated by anything. The force behind transcendental patience is not driven by premature impulse nor by anything else of that nature. It is very slow and sure and continuous, like the walk of an elephant.

Patience also feels space. It never fears new situations, because nothing can surprise the bodhisattva—nothing. Whatever comes—be it destructive, chaotic, creative, welcoming, or inviting—the bodhisattva is never disturbed, never shocked, because he is aware of the space between the situation and himself. Once one is aware of the space between the situation and oneself, then anything can happen in that space. Whatever occurs does so in the midst of space. Nothing takes place "here" or "there" in terms of relationship or battle. Therefore transcendental patience means that we have a flowing relationship with the world, that we do not fight anything.

Energy

And then we could go to the next stage, the paramita of energy, *virya*, which is the kind of energy that immediately leads us into situations so that we never miss a chance, never miss an opportunity. In other words, it is joy, joyous energy, as Shantideva points out in his *Bodhisattva-charyavatara*. This energy is joy, rather than the kind of energy with which we work hard because we feel we must. It is joyous energy because we are completely interested in the creative patterns of our lives. One's whole life is opened by generosity, activated by morality, strengthened by patience, and now one arrives at the next stage, that of joy. One never sees situations as uninteresting or stagnant at all, because the bodhisattva's view of life is extremely open-minded, intensely interested. He never evaluates; though that does not mean that he becomes a complete blank. It does not mean that he is absorbed into a "higher consciousness," the "highest state of samadhi," so that he cannot differentiate day from night or breakfast from lunch. It does not mean he becomes vague or wooly-minded. Rather, he actually sees verbalized and conceptualized values as they are, and then he sees beyond concept and evaluation. He sees the sameness of these little distinctions that we make. He sees situations from a panoramic point of view and therefore takes a great deal of interest in life as it is. So the bodhisattva does not strive at all; he just lives.

He takes a vow when he enters the Bodhisattva Path that he will not attain enlightenment until he has helped all sentient beings to attain the awakened state of mind or Buddhahood before him. Beginning with such a noble act of giving, of opening, of sacrifice, he continues to follow this path, taking tremendous interest in everyday situations, never tiring of working with life. This is virya, working hard with joy. There is tremendous energy in realizing that we have given up trying to become the Buddha, that now we have the time to really live life, that we have gone beyond neurotic speed.

Interestingly, although the bodhisattva has taken a vow not to attain enlightenment, because he is so precise and accurate, he never wastes one second. He always lives life thoroughly and fully, and the result is that, before he realizes where he is, he has attained enlightenment. But his unwillingness to attain enlightenment continues, strangely enough, even after he has reached Buddhahood. Then compassion and wisdom really burst out, reinforcing his energy and conviction. If we never tire of situations, our energy is joyous. If we are completely open, fully awake to life, there is never a dull moment. This is virya.

Meditation

The next paramita is *dhyana* or meditation. There are two types of dhyana. The first is that of the bodhisattva, where because of his compassionate energy, he experiences continual panoramic awareness. Dhyana literally means "awareness," being in a state of "awake." But this does not only mean the practice of meditation in a formal sense. The Bodhisattva never seeks a trance state, bliss, or absorption. He is simply awake to life situations as they are. He is particularly aware of the continuity of meditation with generosity, morality, patience and energy. There is a continual feeling of "awake."

The other type of dhyana is the concentration practice of the realm of the gods. The main difference between that type of meditation and the meditation of the bodhisattva is that the bodhisattva does not dwell upon anything, although he deals with actual physical life situations. He does not set up a central authority in his meditation, does not watch himself acting or meditating, so that his action is always meditation and his meditation is always action.

Knowledge

The next paramita is *prajna* or "knowledge." Prajna is traditionally symbolized by a sharp, two-edged sword which cuts through all confusion. Even if the bodhisattva has perfected the other five paramitas, lacking prajna the other actions are incomplete. It is said in the *sutras* that the five paramitas are like five rivers flowing into the ocean of prajna. It also says in the sutras that the *chakravartin* or universal emperor goes to war at the head of four different armies. Without the emperor to lead them, the armies have no direction. In other words, prajna is the intelligence, the basic pattern into which all these other virtues lead and dissolve. It is that which cuts through the conceptualized versions of bodhisattva action—generosity, discipline, and all the rest. The bodhisattva might perform his actions methodically and properly, but without knowledge, without the sword that cuts through doubt and hesitation his action is not really transcendental at all. Thus prajna is intelligence, the all-seeing eye, the opposite of the ego's watching itself doing everything.

The bodhisattva transmutes the watcher or ego into discriminating knowledge, prajna paramita. "Pra" means "super," "jna" means "knowing": super-knowledge, complete, accurate knowledge which sees everything. Consciousness fixed on "this" and "that" has been cut through, which produces the two-fold knowledge, the prajna of knowing and the prajna of seeing.

The prajna of knowing deals with the emotions. It is the cutting through of conflicting emotions—the attitudes that one has toward oneself—thereby revealing what one is. The prajna of seeing is the transcendence of primitive preconceptions of the world. It is seeing situations as they are. Therefore the prajna of seeing allows for dealing with situations in as balanced a way as possible. Prajna completely cuts through any kind of awareness which has the slightest inclination towards separating "that" and "this." This is the reason why the blade is two-edged. It does not just cut in *this* direction, but in *that* one as well. The bodhisattva no longer experiences the irritating quality that comes from distinguishing between *this* and *that*. He just sails through situations without needing to check back. So all the six paramitas are interdependent.

Q: Would you define meditation as simply paying attention to what you're doing, as being mindful?

A: Dhyana, the fifth paramita, is just being aware, being mindful. But dhyana or any of the other paramitas cannot exist independently without transcendental knowledge, prajna. Prajna throws the practice of awareness into a completely different light, transforms it into something more than simple concentration, the one-pointed practice of keeping the mind focused on a particular object or thing. With prajna, meditation becomes awareness of the whole environment of the particular situation you are in. It also results in precision and openness as well, so that you are aware of every moment, every step, every movement you make. And this precision, this simplicity expands into an overall awareness of the entire situation. So meditation is not a matter of dwelling upon one thing, but it means being awake to the whole situation, as well as experiencing the simplicity of events. Meditation is not merely awareness practice alone, because if you only practice awareness, then you do not develop the intuitive insight necessary to expand your practice. Then you have to shift awareness from one subject to another.

Developing prajna is like learning to walk. You might have to begin by developing awareness of just one thing and then develop awareness of two things, and then three, four, five, six and so on. But finally, if you are to walk properly, you must learn to expand your awareness to include the entire situation you are in so that there is one awareness of everything in the same situation. In order to do this it is necessary not to dwell on anything; then you are aware of everything.

Q: If you have conflicts with other people, making it difficult to relate to them, what do you do?

A: Well, if your desire to communicate, which is generosity, is strong, then you have to apply prajna, knowledge, to discover why you are unable to communicate. Perhaps your communication is only one-directional. Perhaps you are unwilling for communication to come from the other direction as well. Perhaps you have a great desire to communicate and put all your energy into your communication. This is a very intense approach, overwhelming for the person to whom you are communicating. They have no room to communicate back to you. You do this with all good intentions, of course, but we have to be careful to see the whole situation, rather than just being keen to throw something at the other person. We must learn to see from the other person's point of view as well. Essentially, we have to provide some kind of space and openness. The urge to convert the other person into our way of thinking is quite difficult to resist; we often experience it. But we must be careful that our communication doesn't become too heavy-handed. And the only way to do this is by learning how to provide space and openness.

Q: What makes us give up desire?
A: The discovery of the truth, the hard fact that you cannot become a bodhisattva unless you give up wanting to become anything. It is not a matter of playing games with yourself. You simply have to surrender. You have to really open and give up. Once you have had some glimpse of what it would be like to surrender, then there is inspiration to go beyond that, to go further. Once you have experienced a tiny glimpse of the awakened state of mind, just a fraction-of-a-second glimpse, there is tremendous desire and effort to proceed on the path. And then one also realizes that in order to go further one must give up altogether the idea of going. The Bodhisattva Path is

divided into ten stages and five paths. At the end of the last path, at the tenth stage, you have a sudden glimpse that you are about to give birth to the awakened state of mind, that you are just about to click into it, when something pulls you back. Then you realize that the only thing holding you back is that you have to give up trying. That is the vajra-like samadhi, the death of desire.

Q: In normal life, not caring is associated with boredom. If, as with the bodhisattva, one doesn't care, then will one be a vegetable?

A: Not caring does not mean becoming a stone or jelly-fish; there is still energy. But from the point of view of a person who cares, if we experience desire or anger but do not act them out and instead try to keep ourselves cool, if we do not put our energy into action, we feel let down, cheated, stifled. This is a one-sided view of energy.

Energy does not at all manifest itself purely in terms of being destructive or possessive. There are further energies which are not at all connected with love or hate. These are the energies of precision, of clarity, of seeing through situations. There are energies of intelligence which arise continuously and which we do not allow ourselves to experience properly. We always regard energy in terms of being destructive or possessive. There is something more than that. There is never a dull moment if you are actually in touch with reality as it is. The spark of energy arises all the time which transcends ignorance and the simple-minded one-directional way.

Q: But how does one know how and where to direct the energy?

A: Because you see situations very clearly, much more clearly than you did before, because you see them as they really are, you know how and where to direct the energy. Previously you imposed your version of reality onto life, rather than seeing things as they are. So when this kind of veil is removed, you see the situation as it is. Then you can communicate with it properly and fully. You do not have to force yourself to do anything at all. There is a continual exchange, a continual dance. It is similar to the sun shining and plants growing. The sun has no desire to create the vegetation; plants simply react to sunlight and the situation develops naturally.

Q: Spontaneously?

A: Spontaneously. Therefore it is accurate, as in the case of causing vegetables to grow; it is very scientific, right on the point. So your actions become exceedingly accurate because they are spontaneous.

Q: Do situations ever call for aggressive action?

A: I don't think so, because aggressive action is generally connected with defending oneself. If the situation has the quality of nowness, of precision, it never gets out of hand. Then there is no need to control it, to defend oneself.

Q: I'm thinking of Christ chasing the money lenders out of the temple.

A: I would not say that was aggressive action; that was truthful action, which is very beautiful. It occurred because he saw the precision of the situation without watching himself or trying to be heroic. We need action like that.

Q: How do we make the transition between a calm, passive

state of mind that lets everything in and a more active, discriminating state of mind?

A: I think the point is to look at it in a completely different way. In fact I do not think our version of everyday life is as precise and accurate and sharp as we generally think it is. Actually we are completely confused, because we don't do one thing at a time. We do one thing and our mind is occupied with a hundred other things, which is being terribly vague. We should approach everyday life in a wholly different manner. That is, we should allow the birth of an intuitive insight which really sees things as they are. The insight at the beginning might be rather vague, only a glimpse of what is, a very small glimmer compared with the darkness of the confusion. But as this kind of intelligence becomes more active and penetrating, the vagueness begins to be pushed aside and dissolves.

Q: Doesn't seeing things as they are require an understanding of the subject, the perceiver, as well as of the object?

A: Yes, that is an interesting point. Somehow you have to be right in no-man's land in order to see things as they are. Seeing things as they are requires a leap, and one can only take this so-called leap without leaping from anywhere. If you see from somewhere, you will be conscious of the distance and conscious of the seer as well. So you can only see things as they are in the midst of nowhere. Like one cannot taste one's own tongue. Think about it.

Q: You speak of only being able to see things as they are from the midst of nowhere. Yet the Buddhist scriptures talk of crossing to the other shore of the river. Could you clarify this?

A: It is something of a paradox, like the idea of leaping from nowhere. Certainly the Buddhist scriptures speak of crossing to the other shore of the river. But you only arrive at the other shore when you finally realize that there is no other shore. In other words, we make a journey to the "promised land," the other shore, and we have arrived when we realize that we were there all along. It is very paradoxical.

Shunyata

Cutting through our conceptualized versions of the world with the sword of prajna, we discover shunyata—nothingness, emptiness, voidness, the absence of duality and conceptualization. The best known of the Buddha's teachings on this subject are presented in the *Prajnaparamita-hridaya*, also called the *Heart Sutra*; but interestingly in this sutra the Buddha hardly speaks a word at all. At the end of the discourse he merely says, "Well said, well said," and smiles. He created a situation in which the teaching of shunyata was set forth by others, rather than himself being the actual spokesman. He did not impose his communication but created the situation in which teaching could occur, in which his disciples were inspired to discover and experience shunyata. There are twelve styles of presenting the dharma and this is one of them.

This sutra tells of Avalokiteshvara, the bodhisattva who represents compassion and skillful means, and Shariputra, the great arhat who represents prajna, knowledge. There are certain differences between the Tibetan and Japanese translations and the Sanskrit original, but all versions make the point that Avalokiteshvara was compelled to awaken to shunyata by the overwhelming force of prajna. Then Avalokiteshvara spoke with Shariputra, who represents the scientific-minded person or precise knowledge. The teachings of the Buddha were put under Shariputra's microscope, which is to say that these teachings were not accepted on blind faith but were examined, practiced, tried and proved.

Avalokiteshvara said: "Oh Shariputra, form is empty, emptiness is form; form is no other than emptiness, emptiness is no other than form." We need not go into the details of their discourse, but we can examine this statement about form and emptiness, which is the main point of the sutra. And so we should be very clear and precise about the meaning of the term "form."

Form is that which *is* before we project our concepts onto it. It is the original state of "what is here," the colorful, vivid, impressive, dramatic, aesthetic qualities that exist in every situation. Form could be a maple leaf falling from a tree and landing on a mountain river; it could be full moonlight, a gutter in the street or a garbage pile. These things are "what is," and they are all in one sense the same: they are all forms, they are all objects, they are just what is. Evaluations regarding them are only created later in our minds. If we really look at these things as they are, they are just forms.

So form is empty. But empty of what? Form is empty of our preconceptions, empty of our judgments. If we do not evaluate and categorize the maple leaf falling and landing on the stream as opposed to the garbage heap in New York, then they are *there*, what *is*. They are empty of preconception. They are precisely what they are, of course! Garbage is garbage, a maple leaf is a maple leaf, "what is" is "what is." Form is empty if we see it in the absence of our own personal interpretations of it.

But emptiness is also form. That is a very outrageous remark. We thought we had managed to sort everything out, we thought we had managed to see that everything is the "same" if we take out our preconceptions. That made a beautiful picture: everything bad and everything good that we see are both good. Fine. Very smooth. But the next point is that emptiness is also form, so we have to re-examine. The emptiness of the maple leaf is also form; it is not really empty. The emptiness of the garbage heap is also form. To try to see these things as empty is also to clothe them in concept. Form comes back. It was too easy, taking away all concept, to conclude that everything simply is what is. That could be an escape, another way of comforting ourselves. We have to actually *feel* things as they are, the qualities of the garbage heap*ness* and the qualities of the maple leaf*ness*, the *isness* of things. We have to feel them properly, not just trying to put a veil of emptiness over them. That does not help at all. We have to see the "isness" of what is there, the raw and rugged qualities of things precisely as they are. This is a very accurate way of seeing the world. So first we wipe away all our heavy preconceptions, and then we even wipe away the subtleties of such words as "empty," leaving us nowhere, completely with what is.

Finally we come to the conclusion that form is just form and emptiness is just emptiness, which has been described in the sutra as seeing that form is no other than emptiness, emptiness is no other than form; they are indivisible. We see that looking for beauty or philosophical meaning to life is merely a way of justifying ourselves, saying that things are not so bad as we think. Things *are* as bad as we think! Form is form, emptiness is emptiness, things are just what they are and we do not have to try to see them in the light of some sort of profundity. Finally we come down to earth, we see things as they are. This does not mean having an inspired mystical vision with archangels, cherubs and sweet music playing. But things are seen as they *are*, in their *own* qualities. So shunyata in this case is the complete absence of concepts or filters of any kind, the absence even of the "form is empty" and the "emptiness is form" conceptualization. It is a question of seeing the world in a direct way without desiring "higher" consciousness or significance or profundity. It is just directly perceiving things literally, as they are in their own right.

We might ask how we could apply this teaching to everyday life. There is a story that when the Buddha gave his first discourse on shunyata, some of the arhats had heart attacks and died from the impact of the teaching. In sitting meditation these arhats had experienced absorption in space, but they were still dwelling upon space. Inasmuch as they were still dwelling upon something, there was still an experience and an experiencer. The shunyata principle involves not dwelling upon anything, not distinguishing between this and that, being suspended nowhere.

If we see things as they are, then we do not have to interpret or analyze them further; we do not need to try to understand things by imposing spiritual experience or philosophical ideas upon them. As a famous Zen master said: "When I eat, I eat; when I sleep, I sleep." Just do what you do, completely, fully. To do so is to be a *rishi*, an honest, truthful person, a straightforward person who never distinguishes between this and that. He does things literally, directly, as they are. He eats whenever he wants to eat; he sleeps whenever he wants to sleep. Sometimes the Buddha is described as the *Maharishi*, the Great Rishi who was not trying to be truthful but simply was true in his open state.

The interpretation of shunyata which we have been discussing is the view of the *Madhyamika* or "Middle Way"

philosophical school founded by Nagarjuna. It is a description of an experiential reality which can never be accurately
described because words simply are not the experience. Words
or concepts only *point* to partial aspects of experience. In
fact, it is dubious that one can even speak of "experiencing"
reality, since this would imply a separation between the experiencer and the experience. And finally, it is questionable
whether one can even speak of "reality" because this would
imply the existence of some objective knower outside and
separate from it, as though reality were a nameable thing
with set limits and boundaries. Thus the Madhyamika school
simply speaks of the tathata, "as it is." Nagarjuna much pre-
ferred to approach truth by taking the arguments of other
philosophical schools on their own terms and logically reduc-
ing them *ad absurdum*, rather than by himself offering any
definitions of reality.

There are several other major philosophical approaches
to the problems of truth and reality which preceded and influenced the development of the Madhyamika school. These
lines of thought find their expression not only in the earlier
Buddhist philosophical schools but also in the approaches of
theistic Hinduism, Vedantism, Islam, Christianity, and most
other religious and philosophical traditions. From the point
of view of the Madhyamika school, these other approaches
can be grouped together into three categories: the eternalists,
the nihilists, and the atomists. The Madhyamikas viewed the
first two of these approaches as being false, and the third as
being only partially true.

The first and most obvious of these three "misconceptions
of the nature of reality" is eternalism, an approach which is
often that of the more naive versions of theism. Eternalistic
doctrines view phenomena as containing some sort of eternal

essence. Things are born and die, yet they contain an essence which does not perish. The quality of eternal existence must adhere to some *thing*, so the holders of this doctrine usually subscribe to belief in God, a soul, an atman, an ineffable self. Thus the believer asserts that something does exist as solid, ongoing, and eternal. It is reassuring to have something solid to hang onto, to dwell upon, a fixed way of understanding the world and one's relationship to it.

However, eventually the believer in eternalistic doctrines may become disillusioned with a God he has never met, a soul or essence he cannot find. Which brings us to the next and somewhat more sophisticated misconception of reality: nihilism. This view holds that everything is generated out of nothingness, mystery. Sometimes this approach appears as both theistic and atheistic assertions that the Godhead is un-knowable. The sun shines, throws light upon the earth, helps life to grow, provides heat and light. But we can find no origin to life; there is no logical starting point from which the universe began. Life and the world are merely the dance of *maya*, illusion. Things are simply generated spontaneously out of nowhere. So nothingness seems important in this ap-proach: an unknowable reality somehow beyond apparent phenomena. The universe takes place mysteriously; there is no real explanation at all. Possibly a nihilist would say that the human mind cannot comprehend such mystery. Thus, in this view of reality, mystery is treated as a *thing*. The idea that there is no answer is relied upon and dwelt upon as the answer.

The nihilistic approach evokes the psychological attitude of fatalism. You understand logically that if you do some-thing, things happen in reaction to it. You see a continuity of cause and effect, a chain reaction over which you have no control. This chain reactive process springs from the mystery of "nothingness." Therefore, if you murder someone, it was your karma to murder and was inevitable, fore-ordained. For that matter if you do a good deed, it has nothing to do with whether or not you are awake. Everything springs from this mysterious "nothingness" which is the nihilistic approach to reality. It is a very naive view: one leaves everything to mystery. Whenever we are not quite certain of things which are beyond the scope of our conceptualized ideas, then we begin to panic. We are afraid of our own uncertainty and we attempt to fill the gap with something else. The something else is usually a philosophical belief—in this case, the belief in mystery. We very eagerly, very hungrily search for nothingness, surveying every dark corner in our attempts to find it. But we find only the crumbs. We find nothing more than that. It is very mysterious. As long as we continue to look for a conceptual answer there will always be areas of mystery, which mystery is itself another concept.

Whether we are eternalists or nihilists or atomists, we constantly assume that there is a "mystery," something which we do not know: the meaning of life, the origin of the universe, the key to happiness. We struggle after this mystery, trying to become a person who knows or possesses it, naming it "God," the "soul," "atman," "Brahman," "shunyata," and so on. Certainly this is not the Madhyamika approach to reality, though the early Hinayana schools of Buddhism to some extent fell into this trap, which is why their approach is considered only a partial truth.

The Hinayana approach to reality sees impermanence as the great mystery: that which is born must change and die. However, one cannot see impermanence itself but only its manifestation in form. Thus the Hinayanists describe the universe in terms of atoms existing in space and moments existing in time. As such, they are atomistic pluralists. The Hinayana equivalent of shunyata is the understanding of the transitory and insubstantial nature of form, so Hinayana meditation practice is two-fold: contemplation of the many aspects of impermanence—the processes of birth, growth, decay, and death, and their elaborations; and mindfulness practice which sees the impermanence of mental events. The arhat views mental events and material objects and begins to see them as momentary and atomistic happenings. Thus he discovers that there is no permanent substance or solid thing as such. This approach errs in conceptualizing the existence of entities relative to each other, the existence of "this" relative to "that."

We can see the three elements of eternalism, nihilism, and atomistic pluralism in different combinations in almost all the major philosophies and religions of the world. From the Madhyamika point of view, these three misconceptions of reality are virtually inescapable as long as one searches for an answer to an assumed question, as long as one seeks to probe the so-called "mystery" of life. Belief in anything is simply a way of labeling the mystery. Yogachara, a Mahayana philosophical school, attempted to eliminate this mystery by finding a union of mystery and the phenomenal world.

The main thrust of the Yogachara school is epistemological. For this school the mystery is intelligence, that which knows. The Yogacharyans solved the mystery by positing the indivisible union of intelligence and phenomena. Thus there is no *individual* knower; rather everything is "self-known." There is only "one mind," which the Yogacharyans called "self-luminous cognition," and both thoughts and emotions and people and trees are aspects of it. Thus this school is also referred to in the traditional literature as the *citta-matra* or "mind-only" school.

The Yogachara school was the first school of Buddhist thought to transcend the division between the knower and the known. Thus its adherents explain confusion and suffering as springing from the mistaken belief in an individual knower. If a person believes that he knows the world, then the one mind appears to be split, though actually its clear surface is only muddied. The confused person feels that he has thoughts about and reactions to external phenomena and so is caught in a constant action and reaction situation. The enlightened person realizes that thoughts and emotions on the one hand, and the so-called external world on the other, are *both* the "play of the mind." Thus the enlightened person is not caught in the dualism of subject and object, internal and external, knower and known, I and other. Everything is *self*-known.

However, Nagarjuna contested the Yogacharin "mind-only" proposition and, in fact, questioned the very existence of "mind" altogether. He studied the twelve volumes of the *Prajnaparamita* scriptures, which came out of the second turning of the Wheel of Doctrine by the Buddha, the teaching of the middle portion of his life. Nagarjuna's conclusions are summed up in the principle of "non-dwelling," the main principle of the Madhyamika school. He said that any philosophical view could be refuted, that one must not dwell upon any answer or description of reality, whether extreme or moderate, including the notion of "one mind." Even to say that non-dwelling is the answer is delusory, for one must not dwell upon non-dwelling. Nagarjuna's way was one of non-philosophy, which was not simply another philosophy at all. He said, "The wise should not dwell in the middle either."

Madhyamika philosophy is a critical view of the Yogacharin theory that everything is an aspect of mind. The Madhyamika argument runs: "In order to say that mind exists or that everything is the play of the one mind, there must be someone watching mind, the knower of mind who vouches for its existence." Thus the whole of Yogachara is necessarily a theory on the part of this watcher. But according to the Yogacharyans' own philosophy of self-luminous cognition, subjective thoughts *about* an object are delusive, there being no subject or object but only the one mind of which the watcher is a part. Therefore, it is impossible to state that the one mind exists. Like the physical eye, self-luminous cognition cannot see itself, just as a razor cannot cut itself. By the Yogacharyans' own admission, there is no one to know that the one mind exists.

Then what can we say about mind or reality? Since there is no one to perceive a mind or reality, the notion of existence in terms of "things" and "form" is delusory; there is no reality, no perceiver of reality, and no thoughts derived from perception of reality. Once we have taken away this preconception of the existence of mind and reality, then situations emerge clearly, as they are. There is no one to watch, no one to know anything. Reality just *is*, and this is what is meant by the term "shunyata." Through this insight the watcher which separates us from the world is removed.

How then does belief in an "I" and the whole neurotic process begin? Roughly, according to the Madhyamikas, whenever a perception of form occurs, there is an immediate reaction of fascination and uncertainty on the part of an implied perceiver of the form. This reaction is almost instantaneous. It takes only a fraction of a fraction of a second. And as soon as we have established recognition of what the thing is, our next response is to give it a name. With the name of course comes concept. We tend to conceptualize the object, which means that at this point we are no longer able to perceive things as they actually are. We have created a kind of padding, a filter or veil between ourselves and the object. This is what prevents the maintenance of continual awareness both during and after meditation practice. This veil removes us from panoramic awareness and the presence of the meditative state, because again and again we are unable to see things as they are. We feel compelled to name, to translate, to think discursively, and this activity takes us further away from direct and accurate perception. So shunyata is not merely awareness of what we are and how we are in relation to such and such an object, but rather it is clarity which transcends conceptual padding and unnecessary confusions. One is no longer fascinated by the object nor involved as a subject. It is freedom from *this* and *that*. What remains is open space, the absence of the this-and-that dichotomy. This is what is meant by the Middle Way or Madhyamika.

The experience of shunyata cannot be developed without first having worked through the narrow path of discipline and technique. Technique is necessary to start with, but it is also necessary at some stage for the technique to fall away. From the ultimate point of view the whole process of learning and practice is quite unnecessary. We could perceive the absence of ego at a single glance. But we would not accept such a simple truth. In other words, we have to learn in order to unlearn. The whole process is that of undoing the ego. We start by learning to deal with neurotic thoughts and emotions. Then false concepts are removed through the understanding of emptiness, of openness. This is the experience of shunyata. Shunyata in Sanskrit means literally "void" or "emptiness," that is to say, "space," the absence of all conceptualized attitudes. Thus Nagarjuna says in his *Commentary on Madhya-mika:* "Just as the sun dispels darkness, the perfect sage has conquered the false habits of mind. He does not see the mind or thought derived from the mind."

The *Heart Sutra* ends with "the great spell" or mantra. It says in the Tibetan version: "Therefore the mantra of transcendent knowledge, the mantra of deep insight, the unsurpassed mantra, the unequalled mantra, the mantra which calms all suffering, should be known as truth, for there is no deception." The potency of this mantra comes not from some imagined mystical or magical power of the words but from their meaning. It is interesting that after discussing shunyata —form is empty, emptiness is form, form is no other than emptiness, emptiness is identical with form and so on—the sutra goes on to discuss mantra. At the beginning it speaks in terms of the meditative state, and finally it speaks of mantra or words. This is because in the beginning we must develop a confidence in our understanding, clearing out all preconceptions; nihilism, eternalism, all beliefs have to be cut through, transcended. And when a person is completely exposed, fully unclothed, fully unmasked, completely naked, completely opened—at that very moment he sees the power of the word. When the basic, absolute, ultimate hypocrisy has been unmasked, then one really begins to see the jewel shining in its brightness: the energetic, living quality of openness, the living quality of surrender, the living quality of renunciation.

Renunciation in this instance is not just throwing away but, having thrown everything away, we begin to feel the living quality of peace. And this particular peace is not feeble peace, feeble openness, but it has a strong character, an invincible quality, an unshakeable quality, because it admits no gaps of hypocrisy. It is complete peace in all directions, so that not even a speck of a dark corner exists for doubt and hyprocrisy. Complete openness is complete victory because we do not fear, we do not try to defend ourselves at all. Therefore this is a great mantra. One would have thought that instead of saying, *Om gate gate paragate parasamgate bodhi svaha*, this mantra would say something about shunyata—*Om shunyata maha-shunyata*—or something of the sort. Instead it says, *Gate gate*—"gone, gone, gone beyond, completely gone." This is much stronger than saying "shunyata," because the word "shunyata" might imply a philosophical interpretation. Instead of formulating something philosophical, this mantra exposes that which lies beyond philosophy. Therefore it is *gate gate*—"gone, given up, got rid of, opened." The first *gate* is "rid of the veil of conflicting emotions." The second *gate* represents the veil of primitive beliefs about reality. That is, the first *gate* represents the idea that "form is empty," and the second *gate* refers to "emptiness is form." Then the next word of the mantra is *paragate*— "gone beyond, completely exposed." Now form is form—*paragate*—and it is not only that form is form but emptiness is emptiness, *parasamgate*—"completely gone beyond." *Bodhi*. *Bodhi* here means "completely awake." The meaning is "given up, completely unmasked, naked, completely open." *Svaha* is a traditional ending for mantras which means, "Sobeit." "Gone, gone, gone beyond, completely exposed, awake, sobeit."

Q: How does desire lead to birth?
A: Each time there is a desire there is another birth. You plant wantingness, wanting to do something, wanting to grasp something. Then that desire to grasp also invites something further. Birth here means the birth of further confusion, further dissatisfaction, further wanting. For example, if you

have a great desire for money and you manage to get a lot of it, then you also want to buy something with that money. One thing leads to the next, a chain reaction, so that desire becomes a kind of network. You want something, want to draw something into you, continually.

The experience of shunyata, seeing precisely and clearly what is, somehow cuts through this network, this spider's web, because the spider's web is woven in the space of desire, the space of wanting. And when the space of shunyata replaces it, so to speak, the whole conceptualized formulation of desire is completely eliminated, as though you had arrived on another planet with different air, or a place without oxygen at all. So shunyata provides a new atmosphere, a new environment, which will not support clinging or grasping. Therefore the experience of shunyata also makes impossible the planting of the seed of karma, which is why it is said that shunyata is that which gives birth to all the buddhas, all the awakened ones. "Awakened" means not being involved in the chain reactions and complications of the karmic process.

Q: Why is it that so many of us have such a strong tendency to not see things as they really are?
A: I think largely because we are afraid that we will see it.

Q: Why are we afraid of seeing it?
A: We want an umbilical cord attached to the ego through which we can feed all the time.

Q: Can this understanding of "emptiness is form" be attained through the practice of meditation techniques or must it come to us spontaneously?
A: The perception of shunyata is not achieved through the

practice of mental gymnastics; it is a matter of actually *seeing* it. It could be perceived in sitting meditation or it could be seen in life situations. There is no set pattern to producing it. In the ease of Naropa, the great Indian yogi, he perceived shunyata when his master took off his sandal and slapped him on the cheek. That very moment he saw it. It depends upon the individual situation.

Q: Then it is not something you go looking for?
A: If one is really keen, really devoted to finding it, completely devoted to understanding it, then one has to give up looking for it.

Q: I have some difficulty reconciling the concept of shunyata with what is going on right now.
A: When you have a shunyata experience, it does not mean that you cease to perceive, cease to live on Earth. You still live on the Earth, but you see more precisely what is here. We believe that we know things as they are. But we only see our version which is not quite complete. There is much more to learn about the true subtleties of life. The things we see are a very crude version of what is. Having an experience of shunyata does not mean that the whole world completely dissolves into space, but that you begin to notice the space so that the world is somewhat less crowded. For example, if we are going to communicate to someone, we might prepare ourselves to say such and such to calm him down or explain things to him. But then he comes out with so many complications of his own, he churns out so much himself, that before you know where you are, you are completely confused by him. You share his confusion rather than having the clarity you prepared at the beginning. You have been completely absorbed

into his confusion. So shunyata means seeing through confusion. You keep precision and clarity all the time.

Q: And with this experience, you are still alive in this world?

A: Yes, of course! You see, enlightenment does not mean dying. Otherwise, enlightenment would be a kind of suicide, which is ridiculous. That is the nihilistic approach, attempting to escape from the world.

Q: Is an enlightened person omniscient?

A: I am afraid this is a mistaken conclusion drawn from the Yogacharin one mind theory, a theory which has also appeared in other religious and philosophical traditions. The idea is that an enlightened person has become the one mind and so knows everything that ever was, is or could be. You always get this kind of wild speculation when people involve themselves with "mystery," the unknowable. But I am afraid that there really is no such thing as the one mind.

Q: How is one to begin to see what is?

A: By not beginning, by giving up the idea of a beginning. If you try to affirm a particular territory—my experience— then you are not going to see shunyata. You have to give up the idea of territory altogether. Which can be done, it is not impossible. It is not just philosophical speculation. One can give up the idea of territory, one *can* not begin.

Q: Is it part of not beginning to try for so long that one gives up from exhaustion? Can one give up before one has tried? Is there any shortcut? Must the monkey go through the whole process of banging himself against the walls and hallucinating?

A: I think we must. Sudden enlightenment comes only with exhaustion. Its suddenness does not necessarily mean that there is a shortcut. In some cases, people might experience a sudden flash of enlightenment, but if they do not work their way through, their habitual thought patterns will resume and their minds will become overcrowded again. One must make the journey because, as you said, at the point where you begin to be disappointed you get it.

Q: This seems to lead back to the Hinayana path of discipline. Is that correct?

A: Yes, meditation is hard work, manual work, so to speak.

Q: Having begun, it seems that there is something to do.

A: There is something to do, but at the same time whatever you are doing is only related to the moment rather than being related to achieving some goal in the future, which brings us back to the practice of meditation. Meditation is not a matter of beginning to set foot on the path; it is realizing that you are already on the path—fully being in the nowness of this very moment—now, now, now. You do not actually begin because you have never really left the path.

Q: You described enlightened people as being free from the karmic chain. I would like to know what you meant by that, because it seems to me that they create a new karmic chain.

A: The word "karma" means "creation" or "action"—chain reaction. For example, by looking toward the future we plant a seed in the present. In the case of enlightened people, they do not plan for the future because they have no desire to provide security for themselves. They do not need to know the pattern of the future anymore. They have conquered the preconception of "future." They are fully in the now. The now has the potential of the future in it, as well as that of the past. Enlightened people have completely mastered the restless and paranoid activities of mind. They are completely, fully in the moment; therefore they are free from sowing further seeds of karma. When the future comes they do not see it as a result of their good deeds in the past; they see it as present all the time. So they do not create any further chain reactions.

Q: Is the "awake quality" different from just being in the now?

A: Yes. Enlightenment is being *awake* in the nowness. For instance, animals live in the present and, for that matter, an infant child lives in the present; but that is quite different from being awake or enlightened.

Q: I do not quite understand what you mean by animals and babies living in the present. What is the difference between living in the present in that form and being an enlightened person?

A: I think it is a question of the difference between dwelling upon something and really being in the nowness in terms of "awake." In the case of an infant or animal, it is being in the nowness but it is dwelling upon the nowness. They get some kind of feedback from it by dwelling upon it, although they may not notice it consciously. In the case of an enlightened being, he is not dwelling upon the idea—"I am an enlightened being"—because he has completely transcended the idea

of "I am." He is just fully being. The subject-object division
has been completely transcended.

Q: If the enlightened being is without ego and feels the sor-
rows and the sadness of those around him but does not feel
his own necessarily, then would you call his willingness to
help them get over their difficulties "desire"?
A: I don't think so. Desire comes in when you want to see
someone happy. When that person is happy, then you feel
happy because the activities you have engaged in to make him
happy are, in a sense, done for yourself rather than for the
other person. *You* would like to see him happy. An enlightened being has no such attitude. Whenever someone requires
his help, he just gives it; there is no self-gratification or self-
congratulation involved.

Q: Why did you name your center here Karma Dzong?
A: *Karma* means "action" as well as "Buddha activity,"
and *Dzong* is the Tibetan word for "fortress." Situations just
present themselves rather than being deliberately premeditated. They are perpetually developing, happening quite spontaneously. Also there seems to be a tremendous amount of
energy at the center, which also could be said of karma. It is
energy which is not being misled by anyone, energy which is
in the fortress. What is happening definitely had to happen.
It takes the shape of spontaneous karmic relationships rather
than of missionary work or the conversion of people into
Buddhists.

Q: How would you relate samadhi and nirvana to the concept of shunyata?
A: There is a problem here with words. It is not a matter

of differences; it is a matter of different emphases. Samadhi is complete involvement and nirvana is freedom and both are connected with shunyata. When we experience shunyata, we are completely involved, without the subject-object division of duality. We are also free from confusion.

Prajna and Compassion

In discussing shunyata, we found that we impose our preconceptions, our ideas, our version of things onto phenomena instead of seeing things as they are. Once we are able to see through our veil of preconception, we realize that it is an unnecessary and confused way of attaching handles to experiences without considering whether the handles fit or not. In other words, preconceptions are a form of security. When we see something, immediately we name it and place it in a category. But form is empty; it does not need our categorizations to express its full nature, to be what it is. Form is *in itself* empty of preconception.

But, emptiness is form. This means that at this level of understanding we place too much value on seeing form naked of preconceptions. We would like to experience this kind of insight, as though seeing form as empty were a state we could force our minds to achieve. We search for emptiness so that it too becomes a thing, a form, instead of true emptiness. It is a problem of too much ambition.

Thus, the next stage is for us to give up our ambition to see form as empty. At this point form really emerges from behind the veil of our preconceptions. Form is form, naked form without any philosophical implication behind it. And emptiness is emptiness; there is nothing to hang onto. We have discovered the experience of non-duality.

Nevertheless, having realized that form is form and emptiness is emptiness, we still appreciate our insight into non-duality. There is still a sense of the knower, the experiencer of the insight. There is an awareness that something has been removed, something is absent. Subtly, we dwell on non-duality. Here we enter into a transitional phase between the Mahayana Path and Tantra in which prajna is a continuous experience and compassion is no longer deliberate. But there is still some self-consciousness, some sense of perceiving our own prajna and compassion, some sense of checking and appreciating our actions.

As we discussed in the talk on bodhisattva action, prajna is a very clear, precise and intelligent state of being. It has a sharp quality, the ability to penetrate and reveal situations. Compassion is the open atmosphere in which prajna sees. It is an open awareness of situations which triggers action informed by the eye of prajna. Compassion is very powerful, but it must be directed by the intelligence of prajna, just as intelligence needs the atmosphere of the basic openness of compassion. The two must come simultaneously.

Compassion contains fundamental fearlessness, fearlessness without hesitation. This fearlessness is marked by tremendous generosity, in contrast to the fearlessness of exerting one's power over others. This "generous fearlessness" is the fundamental nature of compassion and transcends the animal instinct of ego. Ego would like to establish its territory, whereas compassion is completely open and welcoming. It is a gesture of generosity which excludes no one.

Compassion begins to play a part in the practice of meditation when you experience, not only calm and peace, but also

warmth. There is a great feeling of warmth which gives rise
to an attitude of openness and welcoming. When this feeling
arises, there is no longer any anxiety or fear that external
agents will act as obstacles to your practice of meditation.

This instinctive warmth, which is developed in meditation
practice, also extends into the post-meditation experience of
awareness. With this kind of true awareness you cannot divorce
yourself from your activity. To do so would be impossible.
If you try to concentrate upon your action—making a cup of
tea or any daily-life activity—and at the same time try to be
aware, you are living in a dream-state. As one of the great
Tibetan teachers said, "Trying to combine awareness and
action in an unskillful way is like trying to mix oil and water."
True awareness must be open rather than cautious or protective. It is open-mindedness, experiencing the open space within
a situation. You may be working, but awareness could also
operate within the context of your work, which then would
be the practice of compassion and meditation.

Generally awareness is absent in our lives; we are completely absorbed in whatever we are doing and we forget the
rest of the environment, we seal it off. But the positive force
of compassion and prajna is open and intelligent, sharp and
penetrating, giving us a panoramic view of life which reveals
not only specific actions and events but their whole environments as well. This creates the right situation for communication with other people. In dealing with other people, we must
not only be aware of what they are saying, but we must also
be open to the whole tone of their being. A person's actual
words and smile represent only a small fraction of his communication. What is equally important is the quality of his
presence, the way he presents himself to us. This communicates much more than words alone.

When a person is both wise and compassionate, his actions are very skillful and radiate enormous energy. This skillful action is referred to as *upaya*, "skillful means." Here "skillful" does not mean devious or diplomatic. Upaya just happens in response to a situation. If a person is totally open, his response to life will be very direct, perhaps even outrageous from a conventional point of view, because "skillful means" does not allow any nonsense. It reveals and deals with situations as they are: it is extremely skillful and precise energy. If the coverings and masks we wear were suddenly to be torn away by this energy, it would be extremely painful. It would be embarrassing because we would find ourselves with nothing on, naked. At such a moment this kind of openness and directness, the outrageously blunt nature of prajna and compassion, might seem extremely cold and impersonal.

To the conventional way of thinking, compassion simply means being kind and warm. This sort of compassion is described in the scriptures as "grandmother's love." You would expect the practitioner of this type of compassion to be extremely kind and gentle; he would not harm a flea. If you need another mask, another blanket to warm yourself, he will provide it. But true compassion is ruthless, from ego's point of view, because it does not consider ego's drive to maintain itself. It is "crazy wisdom." It is totally wise, but it is crazy as well, because it does not relate to ego's literal and simpleminded attempts to secure its own comfort.

The logical voice of ego advises us to be kind to other people, to be good boys and girls and lead innocent little lives. We work at our regular jobs and rent a cozy room or apartment for ourselves; we would like to continue in this way, but suddenly something happens which tears us out of our secure little nest. Either we become extremely depressed or something outrageously painful occurs. We begin to wonder why heaven has been so unkind. "Why should God punish me? I have been a good person, I have never hurt a soul." But there is something more to life than that.

What are we trying to secure? Why are we so concerned to protect ourselves? The sudden energy of ruthless compassion severs us from our comforts and securities. If we were never to experience this kind of shock, we would not be able to grow. We have to be jarred out of our regular, repetitive and comfortable life-styles. The point of meditation is not merely to be an honest or good person in the conventional sense, trying only to maintain our security. We must begin to become compassionate and wise in the fundamental sense, open and relating to the world as it is.

Q: Could you discuss the basic difference between love and compassion and in what relation they stand to each other? A: Love and compassion are vague terms; we can interpret them in different ways. Generally in our lives we take a grasping approach, trying to attach ourselves to different situations in order to achieve security. Perhaps we regard someone as our baby, or, on the other hand, we might like to regard ourselves as helpless infants and leap into someone's lap. This lap might belong to an individual, an organization, a community, a teacher, any parental figure. So-called "love" relationships usually take one of these two patterns. Either we are being fed by someone or we are feeding others. These are false, distorted kinds of love or compassion. The urge to commitment—that we would like to "belong," be someone's child, or that we would like them to be our child—is seemingly powerful. An individual or organization or institution or anything could become our infant; we would nurse it, feed it milk, encourage its growth. Or else the organization is the great mother by which we are continuously fed. Without our "mother" we cannot exist, cannot survive. These two patterns apply to any life energy which has the potential to entertain us. This energy might be as simple as a casual friendship or an exciting activity we would like to undertake, and it might be as complicated as marriage or our choice of career. Either we would like to control the excitement or we would like to become a part of it.

However, there is another kind of love and compassion, a third way. Just be what you are. You do not reduce yourself to the level of an infant nor do you demand that another person leap into your lap. You simply be what you are in the world, in life. If you can be what you are, external situations will become as they are, automatically. Then you can communicate directly and accurately, not indulging in any kind of nonsense, any kind of emotional or philosophical or psychological interpretation. This third way is a balanced way of openness and communication which automatically allows tremendous space, room for creative development, space in which to dance and exchange.

Compassion means that we do not play the game of hypocrisy or self-deception. For instance, if we want something from someone and we say, "I love you," often we are hoping that we will be able to lure them into our territory, over to our side. This kind of proselytizing love is extremely limited. "You should love me, even if you hate me, because I am filled with love, am high on love, am completely intoxicated!" What does it mean? Simply that the other person should march into your territory because you say that you love him, that you are not going to harm him. It is very fishy. Any intelligent person is not going to be seduced by such a ploy.

"If you really love me as I am, why do you want me to enter your territory? Why this issue of territory and demands at all? What do you want from me? How do I know, if I do march into your 'loving' territory, that you aren't going to dominate me, that you won't create a claustrophobic situation with your heavy demands for love?" As long as there is territory involved with a person's love, other people will be suspicious of his "loving" and "compassionate" attitude. How do we make sure, if a feast is prepared for us, that the food is not dosed with poison? Does this openness come from a centralized person, or is it total openness?

The fundamental characteristic of true compassion is pure and fearless openness without territorial limitations. There is no need to be loving and kind to one's neighbors, no need to speak pleasantly to people and put on a pretty smile. This little game does not apply. In fact it is embarrassing. Real openness exists on a much larger scale, a revolutionarily large and open scale, a universal scale. Compassion means for you to be as adult as you are, while still maintaining a childlike quality. In the Buddhist teachings the symbol for compassion, as I have already said, is one moon shining in the sky while its image is reflected in one hundred bowls of water. The moon does not demand, "If you open to me, I will do you a favor and shine on you." The moon just shines. The point is not to want to benefit anyone or make them happy. There is no audience involved, no "me" and "them." It is a matter of an open gift, complete generosity without the relative notions of giving and receiving. That is the basic openness of compassion: opening without demand. Simply be what you are, be the master of the situation. If you will just "be," then life flows around and through you. This will lead you into working and communicating with someone, which of course demands tremendous warmth and openness. If you can afford to be what you are, then you do not need the "insurance policy" of trying to be a good person, a pious person, a compassionate person.

Q: This ruthless compassion sounds cruel.
A: The conventional approach to love is like that of a father who is extremely naive and would like to help his children satisfy all their desires. He might give them everything: money, drink, weapons, food, anything to make them happy. However, there might be another kind of father who would not merely try to make his children happy, but who would work for their fundamental health.

Q: Why would a truly compassionate person have any concern with giving anything?
A: It is not exactly giving but opening, relating to other people. It is a matter of acknowledging the existence of other people as they are, rather than relating to people in terms of a fixed and preconceived idea of comfort or discomfort.

Q: Isn't there a considerable danger of self-deception involved with the idea of ruthless compassion? A person might think he is being ruthlessly compassionate, when in fact he is only releasing his aggressions.
A: Definitely, yes. It is because it is such a dangerous idea that I have waited until now to present it, after we have discussed spiritual materialism and the Buddhist path in general and have laid a foundation of intellectual understanding. At the stage of which I am speaking, if a student is to actually practice ruthless compassion, he must have already gone through a tremendous amount of work: meditation, study,

cutting through, discovering self-deception and sense of humor, and so on. After a person has experienced this process, made this long and difficult journey, then the next discovery is that of compassion and prajna. Until a person has studied and meditated a great deal, it would be extremely dangerous for him to try to practice ruthless compassion.

Q: Perhaps a person can grow into a certain kind of openness, compassion with regard to other people. But then he finds that even this compassion is still limited, still a pattern. Do we always rely on our openness to carry us through? Is there any way to make sure we are not fooling ourselves?

A: That is very simple. If we fool ourselves at the beginning, there will be some kind of agreement that we automatically make with ourselves. Surely everyone has experienced this. For instance, if we are speaking to someone and exaggerating our story, before we even open our mouths we will say to ourselves, "I know I am exaggerating, but I would like to convince this person." We play this little game all the time. So it is a question of really getting down to the nitty-gritty of being honest and fully open with ourselves. Openness to other people is not the issue. The more we open to ourselves, completely and fully, then that much more openness radiates to others. We really know when we are fooling ourselves, but we try to play deaf and dumb to our own self-deception.

Tantra

After the bodhisattva has cut through fixed concepts with the sword of prajna, he comes to the understanding that "form is form, emptiness is emptiness." At this point he is able to deal with situations with tremendous clarity and skill. As he journeys still further along the Bodhisattva Path, prajna and compassion deepen and he experiences greater awareness of intelligence and space and greater awareness of peace. Peace in this sense is indestructible, tremendously powerful. We cannot be truly peaceful unless we have the invincible quality of peace within us; a feeble or temporary peacefulness could always be disturbed. If we try to be kind and peaceful in a naive way, encountering a different or unexpected situation might interfere with our awareness of peace because that peace has no strength in it, has no character. So peace must be stable, deep-rooted and solid. It must have the quality of earth. If we have power in ego's sense, we tend to exert that power and use it as our tool to undermine others. But as bodhisattvas we do not use power to undermine people; we simply remain peaceful.

Finally we reach the tenth and last stage of the Bodhisattva Path: the death of shunyata and the birth into "luminosity." Shunyata as an experience falls away, exposing the luminous quality of form. Prajna transforms into jnana or "wisdom." But wisdom is still experienced as an external discovery. The powerful jolt of the *vajra-like samadhi* is necessary to bring the bodhisattva into the state of *being* wisdom rather than *knowing* wisdom. This is the moment of bodhi or "awake," the entrance into Tantra. In the awakened state the colorful, luminous qualities of the energies become still more vivid.

If we see a red flower, we not only see it in the absence of ego's complexity, in the absence of preconceived names and forms, but we also see the brilliance of that flower. If the filter of confusion between us and the flower is suddenly removed, automatically the air becomes quite clear and vision is very precise and vivid.

While the basic teaching of Mahayana Buddhism is concerned with developing prajna, transcendental knowledge, the basic teaching of Tantra is connected with working with energy. Energy is described in the *Kriyayoga Tantra of Vajramala* as "that which abides in the heart of all beings, self-existing simplicity, that which sustains wisdom. This indestructible essence is the energy of great joy; it is all-pervasive, like space. This is the dharma body of non-dwelling." According to this tantra, "This energy is the sustainer of the primordial intelligence which perceives the phenomenal world. This energy gives impetus to both the enlightened and the confused states of mind. It is indestructible in the sense of being constantly ongoing. It is the driving force of emotion and thought in the confused state, and of compassion and wisdom in the enlightened state."

In order to work with this energy the yogi must begin with the surrendering process and then work on the shunyata principle of seeing beyond conceptualization. He must penetrate through confusion, seeing that "form is form and emptiness is empty," until finally he even cuts through dwelling upon the shunyata experience and begins to see the luminosity of form, the vivid, precise, colorful aspect of things. At this point whatever is experienced in every day life through sense perception is a naked experience, because it is direct. There is no veil between him and "that." If a yogi works with energy without having gone through the shunyata experience, then it may be dangerous and destructive. For example, the practice of some physical yoga exercises which stimulate one's energy could awaken the energies of passion, hatred, pride and other emotions to the extent that one would not know how to express them. The scriptures describe a yogi who is completely intoxicated with his energy as being like a drunken elephant who runs rampant without considering where he is going.

Tantric teaching surpasses the "looking beyond" bias of the transcendental attitude that "form is form." When we speak of transcendence in the Mahayana tradition, we mean transcendence of ego. In the Tantric tradition we do not speak of going beyond ego at all: it is too dualistic an attitude. Tantra is much more precise than that. It is not a question of "getting *there*" or "being *there*"; the Tantric tradition speaks of being *here*. It speaks of transmutation and the analogy of alchemistic practice is used a great deal. For example, the existence of lead is not rejected but lead is transmuted into gold. You do not have to change its metallic quality at all; you must simply transmute it.

Tantra is synonymous with dharma, the path. The function of Tantric practice is to transmute ego, enabling the primordial intelligence to shine through. The word *tantra* means "continuity." It is like the thread which strings beads together. The thread is the path. The beads are the working basis of Tantric practice: that is, the Five Skandas or the five constituents of ego as well as the primordial potential of the Buddha within oneself, the primordial intelligence.

Tantric wisdom brings nirvana into samsara. This may sound rather shocking. Before reaching the level of Tantra, you try to abandon samsara and strive to achieve nirvana. But eventually you must realize the futility of striving and then become completely one with nirvana. In order to really capture the energy of nirvana and become one with it you need a partnership with the ordinary world. Therefore the term "ordinary wisdom," *thamal-gyi-shepa*, is used a great deal in the Tantric tradition. It is the completely ordinary version of "form is form, emptiness is empty"; it is what is. One cannot reject the physical existence of the world as being something bad and associated with samsara. You can only understand the essence of nirvana by looking into the essence of samsara. Thus the path involves something more than simply going beyond duality, something more than mere non-dualistic understanding. You are able to see the "non-dualisticness," so to speak, the "isness" quality of non-duality. You see beyond the negation aspect of shunyata, the negation of duality. Therefore, the term "shunyata" is not used very much in Tantra. In Tantric tradition tathata, "what is," is used, rather than "shunyata" or "emptiness." The word *ösel* (Tibetan) or *prabhasvara* (Sanskrit), which means "luminosity," is also used a lot rather than "shunyata." You find this reference to the Tantric tradition in the Buddha's last turning of the Wheel of Dharma: instead of saying, "Form is empty, emptiness is form," and so on, he says that form is luminous. Luminosity or prabhasvara is connected with *mahasukha*, the "great joy" or "bliss," the full realization that "emptiness is emptiness." It is not empty simply because form is also form.

The dynamic quality of energy is not expressed enough in

the doctrine of shunyata because the whole discovery of shunyata derives its meaning relative to samsaric mind. Shunyata
offers an *alternative* to samsara and so the teaching of shunyata is directed toward the samsaric mentality. Even if this
teaching goes beyond saying that "form is empty and emptiness is form" to say that "emptiness is no other than form"
and "form is no other than emptiness," still it does not go so
far as to say that form has this energy and emptiness has this
energy. In the *Vajrayana* or Tantric teaching the principle of
energy plays a very important part.

The teaching must connect with the day to day lives of its
practitioners. We are confronted with the thoughts, emotions
and energies of our relationships with other people and the
world. How are we going to relate our understanding of shunyata to everyday events unless we recognize the energy aspect
of life? If we cannot dance with life's energies, we will not be
able to use our experience of shunyata to unite samsara and
nirvana. Tantra teaches not to suppress or destroy energy but
to transmute it; in other words, go with the pattern of energy.
When we find balance going with the energy, we begin to get
acquainted with it. We begin to find the right path with the
right direction. This does not mean that a person has to become a drunken elephant, a wild yogi in the pejorative sense.

A perfect example of going with energy, of the positive wild
yogi quality, was the actual transmission of enlightenment
from Tilopa to Naropa. Tilopa removed his sandal and
slapped Naropa in the face. He used the situation of the moment, Naropa's energy of curiosity and seeking, transmuting
it into the awakened state. Naropa had tremendous energy
and intelligence, but his energy was not related to Tilopa's
understanding, to his openness of mind, which was another
kind of energy. In order to penetrate this barrier a sudden

jolt was needed, a shock which was not artificial. It is like a crooked building which is just about to fall down but is straightened suddenly, accidentally, by an earthquake. Natural circumstances are used to restore the original state of openness. When one goes with the pattern of energy, then experience becomes very creative. The energy of wisdom and compassion is continually operating in a precise and accurate way.

As the yogi becomes more sensitive to the patterns and qualities of energy, he sees more clearly the meaning or symbolism in life experiences. The first half of Tantric practice, the Lower Tantra, is called *Mahamudra*, which means "Great Symbol." Symbol, in this sense, is not a "sign" representing some philosophical or religious principle; it is the demonstration of the living qualities of what is. For instance, in the direct perception of a flower, the perception of naked insight, unclothed and unmasked, the color of the flower conveys a message over and beyond the simple perception of color. There is great meaning in this color, which is communicated in a powerful, almost overwhelming way. Conceptualized mind is not involved in the perception and so we are able to see with great precision, as though a veil had been removed from before our eyes.

Or if we hold a piece of rock in our hands with that clarity of perception which is the direct contact of naked insight, we not only feel the solidity of that one rock, but we also begin to perceive the spiritual implications of it; we experience it as an absolute expression of the solidity and majesty of earth. In fact we could be holding Mount Everest in our hands, as far as the recognition of fundamental solidity is concerned. That small rock represents every aspect of solidness. I do not mean this in the physical sense alone; but I am speaking of solidity in the spiritual sense, the solidity of peace and energy, indestructible energy. The yogi feels the solidity and forbearance of earth—whatever you plant or bury in it, the earth never reacts against it. In this rock he is aware of the enlightened Wisdom of Equanimity as well as the samsaric quality of ego-pride which wants to build a high pyramid or monument to its own existence. Every situation we encounter has this vivid connection with our state of being. It is interesting to note that in the Tantric iconography a number of symbolic figures are shown holding a mountain in one hand, which represents exactly what we have been discussing: solid peace, solid compassion, solid wisdom which cannot be influenced by the frivolity of ego.

Every texture we perceive has some spiritual implication automatically, and we begin to realize the tremendous energy contained within this discovery and understanding. The meditator develops new depths of insight through direct communication with the reality of the phenomenal world. He is able to see not only the absence of complexity, the absence of duality, but the *stoneness* of stone and the *waterness* of water. He sees things precisely as they are, not merely in the physical sense, but with awareness of their spiritual significance. Everything he sees is an expression of spiritual discovery. There is a vast understanding of symbolism and a vast understanding of energy. Whatever the situation, he no longer has to force results. Life flows around him. This is the basic *mandala* principle. The mandala is generally depicted as a circle which revolves around a center, which signifies that everything around you becomes part of your awareness, the whole sphere expressing the vivid reality of life. The only way to experience things truly, fully, and properly is through the practice of meditation, creating a direct link with nature, with life, with all situations. When we speak of being highly developed spiritually, this does not mean that we float in the air. In fact, the higher we go, the more we come down to earth.

It is important to remember that the practice of meditation begins with the penetration of the neurotic thought pattern which is the fringe of ego. As we proceed further, we see through not only the complexity of the thought processes but also the heavy "meaningfulness" of concepts expressed in names and theories. Then at last we create some space between *this* and *that*, which liberates us tremendously. Having created space, we then go on to the Vajrayana practice of creating a direct link with life experience. These three steps are, in essence, the Three Yanas: the Hinayana, the vehicle of method; the Mahayana, the vehicle of shunyata or space; and the Vajrayana or Tantra, the vehicle of direct energy.

In the Tantric tradition energy is categorized in five basic qualities or *Buddha Families*: *Vajra, Ratna, Padma, Karma* and *Buddha*. Each Buddha Family has an emotion associated with it which is transmuted into a particular "wisdom" or aspect of the awakened state of mind. The Buddha Families are also associated with colors, elements, landscapes, directions, seasons, with any aspect of the phenomenal world.

Vajra is associated with anger, which is transmuted into Mirror-like Wisdom. We sense something beyond the cloudy, possessive and aggressive qualities of anger and this intuitive insight enables us to automatically transmute the essence of anger into precision and openness, rather than deliberately changing it.

Vajra is also associated with the element of water. Cloudy, turbulent water symbolizes the defensive and aggressive nature of anger while clear water suggests the sharp, precise, clear reflectiveness of Mirror-like Wisdom.

Vajra is the color white. Anger is the very blunt and direct experience of defending oneself; therefore it is like a sheet of white paper, very flat and opaque. But it also has the potential of luminosity, of the brilliance of reflection which is Mirror-like Wisdom.

Vajra is connected with the East, the dawn, winter. It is a winter morning, crystal clear, icicles sharp and glittering. The landscape is not empty or desolate but is full of all sorts of thought-provoking sharpness. There are many things to intrigue the observer. For example, the ground, trees, plants all have their own way of freezing. Different trees have different ways of carrying snow and different ways of relating to temperature.

Vajra deals with objects in terms of their textures and their relations to each other. Everything is analyzed in its own terms. The intelligence of Vajra never leaves any unexplored areas or hidden corners. It is like water flowing over a flat surface, completely covering the surface but remaining transparent.

Ratna is associated with pride and earth—solidity, mountains, hills, pyramids, buildings. "I am completely secure. I am what I am." It is a very proud way of looking at oneself. This means that one is afraid to loosen up, is continually piling up defenses, building a fortress. Equally, Ratna is the Wisdom of Equanimity, which is all-pervading. Whether you construct buildings out of earth or whether you simply leave the earth as it is, it is the same thing. The earth remains as it is. You do not feel defeated or threatened at all. If you are a proud person, you feel yourself constantly challenged by the possibility of failure and defeat. In the enlightened mind the anxiety of maintaining oneself is transmuted into equanimity. There is still awareness of the solidity and stability of earth but there is no fear of losing it. Everything is open, safe and dignified; there is nothing to fear.

Ratna is related to the South and autumn, fertility, richness in the sense of continual generosity. When fruit is ripe, it automatically falls to the ground, asking to be eaten up. Ratna has this kind of giving away quality. It is luscious and open with the quality of mid-morning. It is yellow, connected with the sun's rays. Where Vajra is associated with crystal, Ratna is gold, amber, saffron. It has a sense of depth, real earthiness rather than texture, whereas Vajra is purely texture, a crispy quality rather than fundamental depth. Ratna is so ripe and earthy, it is like a gigantic tree which falls to the ground and begins to rot and grow mushrooms all over it and is enriched by the weeds growing around it. It is a log in which animals might nest. Its color begins to turn to yellow and its bark to peel off, revealing an interior which is very rich and very solid. If you were to attempt to remove this log in order to use it as part of a garden arrangement, it would be impossible because it would crumble and fall apart. It would be too heavy to carry anyway.

Padma is connected with passion, a grasping quality, a desire to possess. In the background of passion there is the instinct toward union, wanting to be completely one with something. But passion has an hysterical quality, a neurotic quality which ignores the real state of being united and instead wants to possess in order to *become* united. Passion defeats its own purpose automatically. In the case of Discriminating Awareness, which is the wisdom aspect of passion, one sees the quality of "this" and "that" precisely and sharply. In other words, communication takes place. If you are going to communicate with someone, you must respect the existence of the other person as well as your process of communication. Discriminating Awareness Wisdom recognizes the fact of union, which is quite different from dualistically separating "that " from "this" in order to maintain oneself. The consuming quality of burning fire, desire, is transmuted into the wisdom of binding together through communication. You may be completely caught up with possessiveness in a spiritual or material sense. You may want something more than you can have. You may be so fascinated by the exotic qualities of the thing you want that you are blind to the world around you. You are completely wrapped up in desire, which produces an automatic sort of stupidity and ignorance. This ignorance in desire is transcended in Discriminating Awareness Wisdom.

Padma is linked with the West and color red. Red stands out from any other color, is very provocative, draws you towards it. It is also connected with the element of fire. In the confused state fire does not discriminate among the things that it grasps, burns and destroys. In the awake state the heat of passion is transmuted into the warmth of compassion.

Padma is related to early spring. The harshness of winter is just about to soften with the promise of summer. Ice begins to melt, snowflakes become soggy. Padma is very much connected with facade; it has no feeling of solidity or texture; it is purely concerned with colors, the glamorous qualities, sunset. The visual quality of the surface is more important than its being. So padma is involved with art rather than science or practicality.

Padma is a reasonable location, a place where wild flowers grow, a perfect place to have animals roaming about, such as a highland plateau. It is a place of meadows scattered with gentle rocks suitable for young animals to play among.

Karma is associated with the emotion of jealousy, envy, and the element of wind. However, the terms "jealousy" and "envy" are not powerful and precise enough to describe the quality of Karma. "Absolute paranoia" probably is a good phrase. You feel that you are not going to achieve any of your goals. You become irritated by the accomplishments of other people. You feel left behind and cannot bear to see others surpass you. This fear, this distrust of oneself, is connected with the element of wind. Wind never blows in all directions but it blows in one direction at a time. This is the one-way view of paranoia or envy.

Karma is connected with the Wisdom of All-Accomplishing Action. The quality of paranoia falls away but the qualities of energy, keenness to action and openness remain. In other words, the active aspect of wind is retained so that one's activity touches everything in its path. One's action is appropriate because it does not involve self-conscious panic or paranoia anymore. It sees the possibilities inherent in situations and automatically takes the appropriate course. It fulfills the purpose.

Karma suggests summer in the North. It is the efficiency of Karma which connects it with this season, for it is a summer in which all things are active, growing, fulfilling their function. Millions of interconnected actions take place: living things grow, plants, insects, animals. There are thunderstorms and hailstorms. There is the sense that you are never left to enjoy the summer because something is always moving in order to maintain itself. It is a bit like late spring, but it is more fertile because it sees that all things are fulfilled at the right moment. The color of Karma is the green of vegetables

and grasses, of growing energy. Whereas the Karma of summer is still competing, trying to give birth, the Ratna of autumn has tremendous confidence; everything has been accomplished. The mood of Karma is after sunset, dusk, late day
and early night.

Buddha is associated with dullness and has an all-pervading
quality because it contains and goes with all the rest of the
emotions. The active factor in this dullness is the action of
ignoring. Ignoring does not want to see. It just ignores and
overcrowds itself. You are completely relaxed, completely
careless. You would rather maintain your stupor than search
or struggle for anything, and a slothful, stupid quality is
brought to all the other emotions.

The wisdom connected with Buddha is that of All-Encompassing Space. The all-pervading quality of dullness is kept
as the foundation, but the flicker of doubt and sloth in this
dullness is transformed into wisdom. This wisdom contains
tremendous energy and intelligence which run right through
all the other elements, colors, and emotions, which activate all
the rest of the Five Wisdoms.

Buddha is the foundation or the "basic ground." It is the
environment or oxygen which makes it possible for the other
principles to function. It has a sedate, solid quality. Ratna is
very solid and earthy as well, but it is not as earthy as Buddha
which is dull-earthy, uninteresting-earthy. Buddha is somewhat desolate, too spacious. It is a campsite where only the
stones from campfires are left. The place has a sense of having
been inhabited for a long time, but at present no one is there.
The inhabitants were not killed or forced to move violently;
they simply left. The mood is like that of the caves where
American Indians used to live. They have a feeling of the
past, but at the same time there are no outstanding character-

istics. The tone is very dull, quite possibly in the plains, very flat. Buddha is connected with the color blue, the cool, spacious quality of sky.

Q: How do the pictures of Buddhas, *yidams*, wrathful gods and other symbols fit into the Tibetan spiritual path?

A: There is a great deal of misunderstanding regarding Tibetan iconography. Perhaps we should quickly go through the structure of iconography and symbolism in Tantra. There is what is called "the iconography of the guru," which is connected with the pattern of the path, with the fact that, before you start to receive any teaching, you must surrender willingly, must open yourself. In order to surrender you somehow must identify yourself completely with the fullness and richness of life. At this point surrendering is not emptying in the sense of shunyata emptiness, which is a more advanced experience. But in the early stages of the path surrender means becoming an empty vessel. It also means identification with the fullness, with the richness of the teaching. So symbolically the gurus of the lineage wear highly ornamented robes, hats and scepters and have other ornaments which they hold in their hands.

Then there is the iconography of the yidams which is connected with Tantric practice. Yidams are the different aspects of the five Buddha-principles of energy. They are depicted as male *herukas* or female *dakinis* and can be either wrathful or peaceful. The wrathful aspect is associated with transmutation by force, leaping into wisdom and choiceless transmutation. It is the act of cutting through, associated with crazy wisdom. Peaceful yidams are associated with transmutation by "process"; that is, confusion is pacified and gradually worn out.

The yidams wear the costumes of *rakshasas* who in Indian

mythology are vampires connected with Rudra, King of the Maras, the evil ones. The symbolism involved is that, when ignorance, symbolized by Rudra, has created its empire, then wisdom appears and destroys the empire and takes the costumes of its emperor and his retinue. The yidams' costumes symbolize that they have transmuted ego into wisdom. The five-skulled crowns they wear represent the five emotions which have been transmuted into the Five Wisdoms. These emotions are not thrown away but are worn as ornaments. Furthermore, the trident or *trishula* which the yidams carry is ornamented with three heads: a fresh head, a dry shrunken head and a skeleton head. The fresh head represents hot passion. The dry one represents cold anger and toughness, like tough meat. The skeleton head represents stupidity. The trishula is an ornament which symbolizes transcendence of these three impulses. In addition the trident has three points which represent the three basic principles of being: shunyata, energy and the quality of manifestation. These are the three "bodies" of the Buddha, the Three Kayas: Dharmakaya, Sambhogakaya and Nirmanakaya. All the ornaments worn by the yidams—the bone ornaments, snakes and others—are associated with different aspects of the path. For example, they wear a garland of fifty-one skulls which represents transcendence of the fifty-one types of thought patterns discussed in the Hinayana doctrine of *Abhidharma*.

In Tantric practice one identifies with a yidam of a particular Buddha Family corresponding to one's nature. For instance, if a yidam is associated with the Ratna family, then he will be yellow in color and have symbolism characteristic of Ratna. The types of mandalas given to you by your teacher depend upon the family to which you belong, whether you belong to the passionate family or the family of pride, or whether you have the quality of air or water in you. Generally one can feel that certain people have the quality of earth and solidness, and certain people have the quality of air, rushing here and there, and other people have the quality of warmth and a presence connected with fire. The mandalas are given to you so that you can identify yourself with your particular emotions which have the potential of transmuting into wisdom. Sometimes you practice the visualization of these yidams. However, when you begin working with them, you do not visualize them immediately. You begin with an awareness of shunyata and then develop the feeling of the presence of that image or form. Then you recite a mantra which has an association with this particular feeling. In order to weaken the strength of ego, one somehow must establish a link between the imaginary presence and the watcher of oneself, the ego. The mantra is the link. After the practice of mantra, you dissolve the image or the form into a certain color of light appropriate to the specific yidam. Finally you end your visualization with, again, an awareness of shunyata. The whole idea is that these yidams must not be regarded as external gods who will save you, but they are expressions of your true nature. You identify yourself with the attributes and colors of particular yidams and feel the sound that comes from the mantra so that finally you begin to realize that your true nature is invincible. You become completely one with the yidam.

In *Maha Ati*, the highest tantra, the sense of identification falls away and one merges into one's true nature. Only the energies and colors remain. Previously you saw through forms and images and sounds, saw their empty quality. Now you see the forms, images, and sounds in their true quality. It is the idea of returning to samsara which is expressed in the Zen tradition by the Ox-herding pictures: you have no man and no ox, and then at the end, you have return to the world.

Thirdly, there is the iconography of the "protective divinities." In the practice of identifying yourself with a particular yidam you have to develop an awareness which throws you back to your true nature from your confused nature. You need sudden shocks, reminders all the time, an awake quality. This awareness is represented by the protective divinities which are shown in wrathful form. It is a sudden jerk which reminds you. It is a wrathful awareness because it involves leaping. This leap needs a certain kind of energy to cut through confusion. You have to actually take the initiative to leap without any hesitation from the boundary of confusion into openness. You must really destroy hesitation. You must destroy all obstacles you meet on the path. Therefore this divinity is called protective. "Protection" does not mean securing your safety, but it signifies a reference point, a guideline which reminds you, keeps you in your place, in the open. For instance, there is a *Mahakala* protective divinity called Six-Armed Mahakala who is black in color and stands on *Ganesha*, the elephant-headed god who here symbolizes subconscious thoughts. This subconscious gossip is an aspect of slothfulness that automatically distracts you from being aware and invites you back to being fascinated by your thoughts and emotions. It especially plays upon the survey nature of your thoughts—intellectual, domestic, emotional thoughts, whatever they may be. The Mahakala brings you back to openness. The intent of the symbolism is that the Mahakala overpowers subconscious gossip by standing on it. The Mahakala represents the leap into penetrating awareness.

Generally, all Buddhist Tantric iconography is included in these three categories: the guru, the yidams and the protective divinities. The iconography of the guru expresses the richness of the lineage. The yidams allow you to identify with your particular nature. Then there are the protective divinities to act as reminders to you. The yidams and the protective divinities are generally shown in varying intensities of wrath, depending upon the intensity of awareness needed in order for you to see your true nature.

The wrathful yidams are always associated with what is known in Tantric terms as *vajra anger*, the anger which has the tathata quality; in other words, it is anger without hatred, a dynamic energy. This particular energy, whatever Wisdom it may belong to, is invincible. It is completely indestructible, imperturbable, because it is not created but is discovered as an original quality. It is, therefore, not subject to birth and death. It is always depicted as angry, wrathful and warrior-like.

Q: How does transmutation take place?
A: Transmutation takes place with the understanding of shunyata and then the sudden discovery of energy. You realize that you no longer have to abandon anything. You begin to see the underlying qualities of wisdom in your life-situation, which means that there is a kind of leap. If you are highly involved in one emotion such as anger, then by having a sudden glimpse of openness, which is shunyata, you begin to see that you do not have to suppress your energy. You do not have to keep calm and suppress the energy of anger, but you can transform your aggression into dynamic energy. It is a question of how open you are, how much you are really willing to do it. If there is less fascination and satisfaction with the explosion and release of your energy, then there is more likelihood of transmuting it. Once we become involved

with the fascination and satisfaction of energy, then we are
unable to transmute it. You do not have to completely change
yourself, but you can use part of your energy in an awakened
state.

Q: What is the difference between jnana and prajna?
A: One cannot regard wisdom as an external experience.
That is the difference between wisdom and knowledge, jnana
and prajna. Prajna is knowledge in terms of relativity, and
jnana is wisdom beyond any kind of relativity. You are completely one with wisdom; you do not regard it as something
educational or something experiential.

Q: How do you transmute emotion? How do you deal with
it?
A: Well, that is a very personal question rather than an
intellectual one. The whole point is that we have not actually
experienced our emotions, although we think we have. We
have only experienced emotions in terms of me and my anger,
me and my desire. This "me" is a kind of central governing
structure. The emotions play the part of messengers, bureau-
crats and soldiers. Instead of experiencing emotions as being
separate from you, your rather unruly employees so to speak,
you must actually feel the texture and real living quality of
the emotions. Expressing or acting out hatred or desire on
the physical level is another way of trying to escape from
your emotions, just as you do when you try to repress them.
If one actually feels the living quality, the texture of the
emotions as they are in their naked state, then this experience
also contains ultimate truth. And automatically one begins
to see the simultaneously ironical and profound aspects of
the emotions, as they are. Then the process of transmutation,

that is, transmuting the emotions into wisdom, takes place automatically. But, as I have said, it is a personal question; we really have to do it. Until we actually do it, no words can describe it. We have to be brave enough to actually encounter our emotions, work with them in a real sense, feel their texture, the real quality of the emotions as they are. We would discover that emotion actually does not exist as it appears, but it contains much wisdom and open space. The problem is that we never experience emotions properly. We think that fighting and killing express anger, but these are another kind of escape, a way of releasing rather than actually experiencing emotion as it is. The basic nature of the emotions has not been felt properly.

Q: When the emotions are transmuted, that doesn't mean they disappear, does it?

A: Not necessarily, but they are transmuted into other forms of energy. If we are trying to be good or peaceful, trying to suppress or subdue our emotions, that is the basic twist of ego in operation. We are being aggressive towards our emotions, trying forcefully to achieve peace or goodness. Once we cease being aggressive towards our emotions, cease trying to change them, once we experience them properly, then transmutation may take place. The irritating quality of the emotions is transmuted once you experience them as they are. Transmutation does not mean that the energy quality of the emotions is eliminated; in fact it is transformed into wisdom, which is very much needed.

Q: What about sexual tantra? Is that the process of transmuting sexual energy into something else?

A: It is the same thing. When the grasping quality of passion or desire is transformed into open communication, a dance, then the relationship of two people begins to develop creatively rather than being stagnating or being irritating to them.

Q: Does this principle of transmutation apply to *sattvic* and *rajasic* and *tamasic* energy as described in the Hindu tradition? You don't want to take tamasic energy and turn it into rajasic, but you take it and use it.
A: That's right, yes. It is very practical, actually. Generally we tend to prepare too much. We say, "Once I make a lot of money, then I will go somewhere to study and meditate and become a priest," or whatever it is we would like to become. But we never do it on the spot. We always speak in terms of, "Once I do something, then . . ." We always plan too much. We want to change our lives rather than use our lives, the present moment, as part of the practice, and this hesitation on our part creates a lot of setbacks in our spiritual practice. Most of us have romantic ideas—"I'm bad now but one day, when I change, I'll be good."

Q: Is the principle of transmutation expressed in art?
A: Yes. As we all know, similar combinations of colors and patterns have been created by different people from different cultures at different times. Spontaneous, expressive art automatically has a universal quality. That is why you do not have to go *beyond* anything. If you see fully and directly, then *that* speaks, *that* brings some understanding. Choosing a green light for go in traffic and a red light for stop, for danger, suggests some kind of universality in the effect of color.

Q: What about dance and theater?

A: It is the same thing. The trouble is, if you become too self-conscious in creating a work of art, then it ceases to be a work of art. When masters of art are completely absorbed in their work, they produce masterpieces, not because they are aware of their teachers, but because they become completely absorbed in the work. They do not question, they just do it. They produce the right thing quite accidentally.

Q: How is the fear or paranoia that interferes with spontaneity transmuted into action?

A: There are no special tricks involved in overcoming this and overcoming that in order to achieve a certain state of being. It is a question of leaping. When a person actually understands that he is in a state of paranoia, then that implies an underlying deep subconscious understanding of the other side, some feeling of the other aspect of it in his mind. Then he has to really take the leap. How to take the leap is very difficult to explain in words; one simply has to do it. It is rather like suddenly being pushed overboard into a river and discovering that you can swim; you just swim across the river. However, if you were to go back to the river and attempt to practice, you probably would not be able to swim at all. It is a question of spontaneity, of using the current intelligence. One cannot explain taking the leap in words; it is beyond words. But it is something that you will be able to do if you really are willing to do it, if you put yourself in the situation to leap and somehow surrender.

Q: If you are frightened and have a strong reaction to the fear, you are aware of the reaction but don't want to get lost in it, you want to remain conscious. How do you do it?

A: It is a question of first acknowledging that such energy

is there, which is the energy to leap, as well. In other words, instead of running away from fear, one must become completely involved in it and begin to feel the rough and rugged quality of the emotion.

Q: Become a warrior?
A: Yes. At the beginning one might be satisfied with seeing the absurdity of the emotion, which would disperse it. But this is still not enough to effect the transmutation principle of Vajrayana. One must see the "form is form" quality of the emotions. Once you are able to look at the emotions properly, from the point of view of "form is form, emotion is emotion," without your preconceptions attached, once you see the naked quality of the emotions as they are, then you are ready to leap. It does not need much effort. You are already delivered to the leap, so to speak. This does not mean of course that, if you are angry, you go out and commit murder.

Q: In other words, see the emotion as it is instead of involving yourself in a scattered, penetrating reaction to a situation.
A: Yes. You see, we do not actually see emotion properly, although we are completely filled with it. If we follow our emotions and escape them by doing something, that is not experiencing them properly. We try to escape or repress our emotions because we cannot bear to be in such a state. But the Vajrayana speaks of looking properly, directly at the emotion and feeling it, its naked quality. You do not actually have to transmute. In fact, you see the already transmuted quality in the emotions: "form is form." It is very subtle and quite dangerous to just throw about.

Q: How does Milarepa's life fit into the pattern of Tantra?

He does not seem to practice transmutation, but rather, renunciation.

A: Of course, in his life-style Milarepa is a classic example of the yogi-renunciate tradition. But usually, when we think of a renunciate, we think of someone who is trying to escape the "evil" of the "worldly" life. This is not the case with Milarepa at all. He was not trying to suppress his "evil" inclinations by meditating alone in the wilderness. He did not lock himself into retreat. He was not trying to punish himself. His asceticism was simply an expression of his character, just as each of our life-styles is an expression of who we are, determined by our psychologies and past histories. Milarepa wanted to be simple and he led a very simple life.

Certainly there is a tendency on the part of people following a religious path to become other-worldly for awhile, and Milarepa was no exception. But people can do this in the middle of a city. Wealthy people can spend a great deal of money going on a religious "trip." But sooner or later, if a person is going to really connect with the teachings, there must be a return to the world. When Milarepa was meditating in retreat, living very austerely, some hunters appeared by chance and gave him some fresh venison. He ate it and his meditation improved immediately. And later on, when he was hesitating to come down to the cities, some villagers appeared at his cave asking for teachings. He was continually being drawn out of isolation by the seemingly accidental play of life-situations, which one could say is the play of the guru, the universality of guru, which always presents itself to us naturally. We may be sitting in meditation in our New York apartment, feeling very "high" and euphoric, very "spiritual." But then we get up and walk into the streets and someone steps on our toe and we have to deal with that. It brings us down to earth, back to the world.

Milarepa was tremendously involved with the process of transmutation of energies and emotions. In fact, when we read *The Hundred Thousand Songs of Milarepa*, the whole first part of the book is dealing with Milarepa's experience of this process. In "The Tale of Red Rock Jewel Valley" Milarepa had only recently left Marpa to go off and meditate alone. This might be called his "adolescent stage," because he was still involved with reliance upon a personal guru. Marpa was still his "daddy." Having opened and surrendered to Marpa, Milarepa still had to learn to transmute the emotions. He was still clinging to the notions of "good" and "bad," and so the world was still appearing to him in the guise of gods and demons.

In "The Tale of Red Rock Jewel Valley," when Milarepa went back into his cave after having a comforting vision of Marpa, he was confronted with a gang of demons. He tried every way he could think of to get rid of them, all kinds of tactics. He threatened them, cajoled them, he even preached the Dharma to them. But they would not leave until he ceased regarding them as "bad" and opened to them, saw them as they were. This was the beginning of Milarepa's period of learning how to subjugate the demons, which is the same thing as transmuting the emotions. It is with our emotions that we create demons and gods: those things which we don't want in our lives and world are the demons; those things which we would draw to us are the gods and goddesses. The rest is just scenery.

By being willing to accept the demons and gods and goddesses as they are, Milarepa transmuted them. They became dakinis, or the energies of life. The whole first part of *The Hundred Thousand Songs* deals with Milarepa's mastery of transmutation, his growing ability to open to the world as it is, until he finally conquered all the demons in the chapter "The Goddess Tserinma's Attack." In this chapter thousands of demons assemble to terrify and attack Milarepa while he is meditating, but he preaches to them, is open and accepting, willing to offer them his whole being, and they are subjugated. At one point five demonesses, beginning to realize that they cannot frighten Milarepa, sing to him,

> If the thought of demons
> Never rises in your mind,
> You need not fear the demon hosts around you.
> It is most important to tame your mind within . . .[1]

> On the steep path of fear and hope
> They lie in ambush . . .[2]

And later Milarepa himself says, "Insofar as the Ultimate, or the true nature of being is concerned, there are neither Buddhas nor demons. He who frees himself from fear and hope, evil and virtue, will realize the insubstantial and groundless nature of confusion. Samsara will then appear to be the Mahamudra itself . . ."[3]

The rest of *The Hundred Thousand Songs* deals with Milarepa's development as a teacher and his relationships with his students. Toward the end of his life he had completely

[1] Garma C. C. Chang, *The Hundred Thousand Songs of Milarepa*, (New York, 1962), p. 306.
[2] Ibid., p. 307.
[3] Ibid., p. 308.

perfected the transmutation process to the point where he could be called the *Vidyadhara* or "Holder of the Crazy Wisdom." No longer could he be swayed by the winds of hope and fear. The gods and goddesses and demons, his passions and their external projections, had been completely subjugated and transformed. Now his life was a continual dance with the dakinis.

Finally Milarepa reached the "old dog" stage, his highest attainment. People could tread on him, use him as a road, as earth; he would always be there. He transcended his own individual existence so that, as we read his last teachings, there is a sense of the universality of Milarepa, the example of enlightenment.

Index

Abhidharma, 231
abhisheka, 55, 57–9, 97. *See also* initiation
Action, All-Accomplishing. *See* Wisdoms, Five
adhishthana, 64–5
aggression, 98, 104–5, 125, 236; expression of, 48, 87, 107, 182; Vajra and 224–5; in Hell Realm, 138–40, 146; in love, 101–2
alaya-vijnana, 122
ambition, 71–2, 89, 91, 147, 158–9, 207; in meditation, 10–11, 153–5, 161. *See also* struggle
Amitabha, color of, 117
anger. *See* aggression *and* vajra-anger
Animal Realm. *See* Realms, Six
arhats, 187, 190, 194
art, 53–4, 80; transmutation in, 237–38
"as it is", 49, 121, 168–70, 188, 191; surrendering to, 26, 28, 69, 101; in Tantra, 220. *See also* reality *and* tathata
asceticism, 47–8, 83, 240. *See also* disciplines, spiritual *and* renunciation
Asura Loka, 131–2, 142–3. *See also* Realms, Six
atman, 193
atomism, 191–4
Avalokiteshvara, 187–8
avidya, 124. *See also* Skandhas, Five
awakened state, 65, 204–5; discovery of, 4–5, 9, 117, 153, 155, 181, 221; evaluation of, 119; expressions of, 10; and bodhisattva, 170. *See also* bodhi *and* enlightenment
Awareness, Discriminating. *See* Wisdoms, Five
awareness, panoramic, 74–5, 100, 113–4, 167–9; loss of, 197

basic ground, 70–1, 122–4, 229–30. *See also* "being as you are" *and* openness

"being as you are", 20–1, 39, 103–4, 213–4. *See also* openness
"being here", 74, 203–4, 219; difficulty of, 65–70, 72; as focus of meditation practice, 155–7; in therapy, 88–9. *See also* "as it is"
bhumi, 168. *See also* Bodhisattva Path
"big deal", 58, 96, 113–7.
"blackout", 124, 129, 130, 133–4. *See also* ego, development of
bliss, 99, 113–4, 143, 168, 220; irrelevancy of, 74–5; search for, 69–71, 79. *See also* luminosity *and* virya
bodhi, 170, 199, 218. *See also* awakened state *and* Bodhisattva Path
bodhisattva, transcendental activities of, 99, 102–3, 170–8
Bodhisattva Path, 99–103, 158, 167–84; levels of, 170, 180–1, 217–19. *See also* Mahayana
Bodhisattva-charyavatara, 175
Brahman, 193
Buddha, Gautama (Shakyamuni), 26, 48, 160, 162, 164; and daughters of Mara, 119; and Four Noble Truths, 119, 151; and *Heart Sutra*, 187–8, 190; and *shamatha*, 157; and teachings, 19; and Three Lords of Materialism, 8–11
Buddha, three "bodies" of, 231. *See also* dharmakaya; nirmanakaya; *and* sambhogakaya
Buddha Families, Five, 224–32
— *Buddha*, 224, 229–30
— *Karma*, 224, 228–9
— *Padma*, 224, 226–28
— *Ratna*, 224, 225–6, 231
— *Vajra*, 119, 224–5, 226
"Buddha activity", 19, 205. *See also* karma
Buddha nature, 47, 156, 170. *See also* intelligence, basic *and* tathagatagarbha

Buddhahood, 11, 65, 176
Buddhism, approach to spirituality of, 4–11, 121–2; distinctions between Vehicles of, 18–9, 157–8, 168–9, 190–7, 208, 218–9, 224; *Madhyamika* school of, 190–7; *Yogachara* school of, 194–6, 202. *See also* Hinayana; Mahayana; Tantra; *and* Vajrayana

categories, grasping nature of, 6, 14–5, 122, 127–8, 130. *See also* concepts; conceptualization; ego, bureaucracy of; evaluation; form; *and* preconceptions
chakravartin, 177–8
chela, 18
Christ, 101, 182
Christian precepts, 58, 88
Christianity, 6, 191
citta-matra school. *See* Buddhism, yogachara school
clarity, of awakened state, 10; as generosity, 97; of *prajna*, 147; as *shunyata*, 197. *See also* precision
communication, allowing space for, 157, 161–2, 169, 180; compassion as, 98, 146–7, 209; generosity as, 171–2, 180; grasping nature of, 158; pain of, 55, 81–82; surrender as, 28
communication with energy of life, 101, 103, 163, 222–4; with spiritual friend, 39–41, 45, 58, 64–5. *See also* openness *and* surrender
communism, 6
compassion, 97–100, 105–6, 210–5; Bodhisattva of, 187; clarity of, 97; fearlessness of, 100, 107, 208, 213; ruthlessness of, 210–1, 214–5; warmth of, 97, 146–7, 208–9; directed by *prajna*, 208–9. *See also* generosity
Concept. *See* Skandhas, Five
concepts, self-protective nature of, 6–7, 11, 127–8, 130; transcendence of, 163, 164, 217; in *Madhyamika* school, 191
conceptualization, absence of, 122–3, 187–90; avoiding, 72; cutting through, 10, 178, 187, 217–8; self-protective nature of, 127–8, 130, 197; of experience, 116–7; in Hinayana thought, 194. *See also* categories; evaluation; form; *and* preconceptions
confidence, 21, 24, 99, 102, 198
confusion, cutting through, 4, 20, 133, 151, 156, 158–9, 233; reality of, 70, 148; as sense of self, 5, 56, 123, 195. *See also* ego
consciousness, states of. *See* ego; enlightenment; Paramitas, Six; Realms, Six; self-consciousness; *and* Skandhas, Five

dakini, 230, 241–3
Damema, 38
dana, 97–100. *See also* Paramitas, Six
death, 8, 112, 142, 143; awareness of, 134
defense mechanisms. *See* ego, self-preservative quality of *and* security
demons, 46, 241–3
depression, 68–71. *See also* despair *and* disappointment
desire, impulse of, 127, 129, 205; path of, 98, 139–46, 180–1, 199–200; transmutation of, 235–7. *See also* samsara
despair, 38, 95, 98
Deva Loka, 131, 143–5. *See also* Realms, Six
dharma, 17, 25, 26, 47–8, 105, 161, 187, 219. *See also* meditation *and* Truths, Four Noble
dharma, living quality of, 17; misconception of, 161; personal expression of, 47–8; styles of presenting, 187; as absence of aggression, 105; as law of existence, 26; as transmutation of ego, 219. *See also* meditation *and* Truths, Four Noble
Dharma, Wheel of, 151, 195, 220. See *also* Truths, Four Noble
dharma body, 218. *See also* dharmakaya
dharmakaya, 218, 231. *See also* Buddha, three "bodies" of
dhyana, 100, 143–4, 177. *See also* meditation *and* Paramitas, Six
disappointment, 151–3; use of, 5, 25–6, 93, 158–9, 202–3. *See also* suffering
discipline, transcendental. *See* Paramitas, Six *and* shila
disciplines, spiritual; interest in, 3; misuse of, 7, 78–80, 83; purpose of, 47–8, 121–2, 153; and humor, 112–6. *See also* meditation
dissatisfaction. *See* disappointment
divinities, protective, 230–3
dream, as self-deception, 65–69, 130–1, 139
drugs, 7, 78, 80, 137
dualistic meditation, 98, 153–4
duality, absence of; 123, 187–198, 208, 219–21; birth of, 123; dynamics of, 14, 123–48, 187–98; transcending of, 170–8, 105, 219–21
duhkha, 119, 151–2, 159. *See also* suffering *and* Truths, Four Noble

eclecticism as function of spirtual materialism, 15–18, 22, 58, 79–81
ego, bureaucracy of, 15–7, 56, 73, 126–7; development of, 122–48, 196–7; dismantling of, 81, 155, 197, 232; distortions of spiritual path by, 3, 7–8, 13–4, 56, 58–9, 63, 114, 119, 134, 158–9;

Ego (*Continued*)
  myth of, 5, 8–9, 69–70, 122–3, 128,
    148, 168; rugged qualities of, 24–6, 28,
    55, 239; self-preservative quality of, 6,
    10–11, 21, 59–60, 86, 126–7, 200;
    territory of, 60, 73, 142–4, 202, 208,
    212–3; transcendence of, 4–5, 11, 151,
    153, 178, 204–5, 219, 243
ego as pain shield, 5, 6, 56, 68, 80–1, 93,
    126–7, 134; as spiritual advisor, 13–4,
    134
egocentricity, 3, 92–3, 96
egohood, 7–8, 143–5
emotions, cutting through, 178; experi-
    encing reality of, 70, 84, 89, 236, 239;
    self protective nature of, 10–11, trans-
    mutation of, 231–32, 235–39, 241–3; in
    ego's development, 120, 167. See also
    desire; fear; and love
emptiness. See shunyata and space
energy, categories of, 181. See also
    Buddha Families, Five
energy, transcendental. See Paramitas,
    Six and virya
energy, *rajasic*, 237; *sattvic*, 237; sexual,
    236–7; solidification of, 126–9;
    tamasic, 237; transmutation of, 219,
    234–43; as focus in Tantra, 218–3;
    and meditation practice, 9–11; of
    primordial intelligence, 160
enlightenment, avoiding concentration
    upon, 118–9; discovery of, 4–5, 11;
    independent nature of, 4, 113; instant,
    65, 93, 115, 117–118; misconceptions
    of, 202; reverse, 133–4; self, 98; and
    bodhisattva, 176; and Milarepa, 241–3.
    See also awakened state; nirvana; and
    samadhi
eternalists, 191–4, 198
evaluation, grasping nature of, 14–5, 58–
    9, 66–72, 116–7, 172; irrelevancy of,
    20, 187, 163; self-protective mechanism
    of, 127–8, 130–1; spiritual attitude
    toward, 112–5, 164, 188. See also con-
    ceptualization
experience, contrasted to understanding,
    84; examining, 9; holding onto, 65–70,
    73; nature of, 187–91; as self-decep-
    tion, 25–6; of spiritual path, 115
existentialism, 6

faith, 20–1, 95
fatalism, 192–3
fear, 48, 108; transmutation of, 238–9;
    of failure, 142–3; of space, 22, 69–70,
    140. See also paranoia
fearlessness. See compassion, fearless
    aspect of
Feeling. See Skandhas, Five
form, 160, 207–8, 232; birth of, 123–6;
    emptiness of, 188–90, 196; luminosity

of, 220–1; solidity of, 148; in medita-
    tion, 154
Form, Lord of, 5–6, 8, 125. See also
    Materialism, Three Lords of
Formless Gods, Realm of, 143–4. See
    also Realms, Six

games, spiritual, 7, 23, 180, 215. See
    also self-deception
Gampopa, 17
Ganesha, 253
generosity, transcendental. See dana and
    Paramitas, Six
goal, truth of, 151, 153. See also Truths,
    Four Noble
God, 4, 192–3
God Realm. See Deva Loka and Realms,
    Six
Great Vehicle, 99. See also Mahayana
guru, 17–9, 31–50; initiation by, 54–9;
    hunting of, 63; personality cult of,
    44–5; preconceptions of, 23, 31, 39,
    63–5, 91–7; reliance on, 241; sur-
    render to, 23, 28, 37–9, 82–5; uni-
    versality of, 45–6, 50, 240. See also
    initiation and spiritual friend
gymnastics, mental, 9, 154, 200–1

hallucinations, 130–2, 134, 146, 148
"hard way", 77–89
hatred, 127, 130–1
Heaps, Five, 123. See also Skandhas, Five
Heart Sutra, 187, 198
Hell Realm. See Realms, Six
heroism, 78, 83–4, 86
heruka, 69, 230
Hinayana, 203, 224; practices, 98, 155–
    7, 167, 194; thought, 193–4, 231. See
    also Buddhism
Hinduism, 79, 160, 191, 237
Human Realm. See Realms, Six
humor, 111–8, 146, 147–8, 154
Hundred Thousand Songs of Milarepa,
    241–3
Hungry Ghosts, Realm of. See Preta
    Loka and Realms, Six
hypocrisy, 41–2, 46, 117–8. See also
    self-deception

inconography, 117, 187, 213, 223; of
    Buddha Families, 224–30; of guru,
    230, 233–4; of protective divinities,
    233–4; of *yidams*, 230–4
ideology, neurotic use of, 6, 8. See also
    intellect
ignorance, 70, 127–8, 133–4
Ignorance, Birth of, 125. See also
    Skandhas, Five
Ignorance, Self-Observing, 125. See also
    Skandhas, Five
Ignorance-Form. See Skandhas, Five

Ignorance Born Within, 125. *See also* Skandhas, Five
illusion, 49, 122–3, 192
impermanence, Hinayana approach to, 193–4
India, 95; Marpa in, 32–6; meditation of, 153–4; mythology of, 230–1
Indian, American, 79, 105
individual effort, necessity of, 17–8, 26–7, 77–8, 89
individuality, 5–7, 48, 123–5, 240. *See also* ego
initiation, 53–61, 63–5, 91. *See also* abhisheka
inspiration, sources of, 17, 22, 162, 170
instinct, ape, 15, 86, 127, 134. *See also* ego
instinct, awakened state as, 4, 160; use of, 22
intellect, 6–8, 127–8, 141; proper use of 54, 146. *See also* conceptualization
intelligence. *See* Skandhas, Five *and* vidya
intelligence, basic, 25, 46–7, 156, 159–60, 162. *See also* Buddha-nature *and* tathagata-garbha
intelligence, primordial, 109, 127–8, 136, 218–20. *See also* yeshe
Islam, 191

Jealous Gods, Realm of. *See* Asura Loka *and* Realms, Six
jnana, 109, 218, 235. *See also* wisdom, crazy
joy. *See* bliss *and* virya
junkyard, spiritual. *See* eclecticism

Kagyu lineage, 17, 31, 48
Karma. See Buddha Families, Five
karma, law of, 146, 199–200, 203–4, 205; as nihilistic invocation, 192–3
Karma Dzong, 3, 205
karuna, 146–7. *See also* compassion
Kayas, Three, 231
knowledge, experiencing of, 17–8, 35–6, 54
knowledge, transcendental. *See* Paramitas, Six *and* prajna
knowledge as spiritual materialism, 15–7. *See also* eclecticism
Kriyayoga Tantra of Vajramala, 218
kshanti, 100. *See also* Paramitas
Kukuripa, 34–5

lama, 31, 53. *See also* guru *and* spiritual friend
Lesser Vehicle, 157. *See also* Hinayana
"letting be", 9–10, 20, 125–6, 135, 158; necessity of technique for, 153. *See also* openness *and* self-trust
Lokas, Six, 131. *See also* Realms, Six

love, 100–2, 113, 211–3
luminosity, birth into, 217–20

Madhyamika school. *See* Buddhism *and* "middle way"
Maha Ati, 232–3
Mahakala, 233
Mahamudra, 222, 242
Maharishi, 190
mahasukha, 220. *See also* bliss
mahavipashyana meditation. *See* awareness, panoramic
Mahayana, 158; expansiveness of, 99, 168–9; and Tantra, 208, 218–9. *See also* Bodhisattva Path *and* Buddhism
mandala, 69, 223–4; assignment of, 231–2
mantra, 39, 198–9, 232
Mara, daughters of, 58–9, 119, 231
Marpa, 17, 32–40, 45–6, 47–9, 69, 241
materialism, physical, 40, 61
materialism, spiritual. *See* spiritual materialism
Materialism, Three Lords of, 5–11
maya, 192. *See also* illusion
meditation, compassionate aspect of, 97–8, 105, 108–9; difficulty of, 135, 203; discovering awakened state by, 4–5, 9–11, 74, 151, 169; ego's imitation of, 7; experiencing ego by, 15, 161; insignificance of, 115–7; misconceptions of, 9–10, 153; short-circuiting ego by, 21–2, 155; stages in practice of, 224. *See also* dhyana; disciplines, spiritual; Paramitas, Six; samadhi; *and* techniques, spiritual
meditations, types of: concentration, 98, 153–4, 177; *mahavipashyana*, 168, 177; *shamatha*, 154–7; *vipashyana*, 100, 167–8; Tantric, 231–2; upon impermanence, 194
"meeting of two minds", 39, 42, 55, 58–9, 64–5, 77, 91–2. *See also* abhisheka
"middle way", 20, 40, 190–1. *See also* Buddhism, Madhyamika school of
Milarepa, 17, 32, 37–40, 45–6, 239–43
Mind, Lord of, 5, 7–8. *See also* Materialism, Three Lords of
"mind only" school. *See* Buddhism, Yogachara school *and* "one-mind" theory
mind, ordinary, 59. *See also* thamal-gyi-shepa *and* wisdom, ordinary
mind and matter, interrelation of, 79, 163–4
motivation, in the awakened state, 162–3. *See also* ambition
mukti, 113
mystery, belief in, 21, 77–80, 91–2; philosophical belief in, 192–3

Nagarjuna, 190–1, 195, 198

Nalanda University, 32–3
Naropa, 17, 32–7, 40, 69, 96–7, 201, 221
nationalism, 6
neurosis, development of, 129, 148; working with, 9, 118, 151–4, 196–7. *See also* ego
Ngonagpa of Langru, 114–5
nihilism, 191–4, 198, 202
nirmanakaya, 231. *See also* Buddha, three "bodies" of
nirvana, 113, 145, 205–6, 220. *See also* enlightenment *and* samadhi,
non-duality, 207–8, 220. *See also* duality *and* shunyata
non-dwelling, 177, 179, 190–5, 218
non-striving, 71–2, 153, 161, 176. *See also*: "letting be"; struggle; surrender; *and* Truths, Four Noble

"one-mind" theory, 194–6, 202. *See also* Buddhism, Yogachara school
"open way", 91–109, 168–9; compassion of, 96–109. *See also* Bodhisattva Path; Mahayana; *and* openness
openness, loss of, 65–70, 122–4; necessity of spiritual friend for, 83; pain of, 81–2; use of disappointment to achieve, 25, 41–2, 71–2, 91–3
openness and Bodhisattva Path, 99–103, 169–77; and Gautama Buddha, 9, 19, 162; and shunyata, 197–9; as surrender to spiritual friend, 24, 28, 37, 39–46, 55–6, 58–9. *See also* communication; "open way"; initiation; shunyata; space; *and* surrender
openness, transcendental. *See* dhyana *and* Paramitas, Six
ordinariness, as expression of basic sanity, 47–9, 59, 67–9, 92, 116. *See also* non-striving *and* wisdom, ordinary
osel, 220. *See also* luminosity

Padma. See Buddha Families, Five
pain, 8, 111, 119, 134; origin of, 151–3, 162; of unmasking, 55, 71, 81–2, 84; as expression of guru, 50, 89. *See also* "hard way" *and* suffering
paramita, definition of, 170
Paramitas, Six, 99–100, 170–8; interdependence of, 174, 178–9
  —discipline, 100, 170, 173–4. *See also* shila
  —energy, 11, 100, 170, 175–7, 181–2. *See also* virya
  —generosity, 99–100, 170–3. *See also* dana
  —knowledge, 100, 146–7, 168, 177–8, 198. *See also* prajna
  —meditation, 100, 177, 179. *See also* dhyana
  —patience, 100, 170, 174–5. *See also*

kshanti
  See also Bodhisattva Path
paranoia, giving up one's, 102–4, 238; of ego, 4–5, 74, 132, 162; of Karma Family, 228; after self-deception, 93. *See also* neurosis
passion, 141, 226. *See also* desire *and* emotions
path, spiritual. *See* dharma *and* meditation
path, truth of, 151, 153–7, 161. *See also* dharma *and* Truths, Four Noble
patience, 156–59, 161
patience, transcendental. *See* kshanti *and* Paramitas, Six
peace, invincible quality of, 198, 217, 223
perception, 6–7, 122–3, 136–7, 183, 196–7; symbolism of, 163, 222–4. *See also* conceptualization; self, sense of; *and* Skandhas, Five
philosophy as function of spiritual materialism, 14–15. *See also* eclecticism
pleasure, attitudes toward, 147–8; search for, 5–6, 139–42, 152; as expression of guru, 50. *See also* bliss *and* security
prabhasvara, 220. *See also* luminosity
prajna, cutting nature of, 177–8, 187; double nature of, 177–8; and compassion, 208–11, 215; as knowledge of situations, 100, 108, 179–80; as transitoriness of ego, 168. *See also* Paramitas, Six
Prajnaparamita scriptures, 195
Prajnaparamita-hridaya, 187. *See also* Heart Sutra
prayer, 7
precision, loss of, 59–124; meditation on, 155–7, 160, 167–8; of disappointment, 25; as quality of awakened state, 10, 74, 123, 147, 179
preconceptions, dwelling on, 154–5, 164; transcendence of, 178, 198, 207, 239; of guru, 23–5; of spiritual path, 121–2, 158–9
Preta Loka, 132, 139–40. *See also* Realms, Six
pride, spiritual, 4. *See also* ego *and* egohood
projections, 131, 168, 243; illusory union with, 144–5. *See also* Realms, Six
psychotherapy, 7, 14, 88–9

rakshasas, 230–1
Ratna. See Buddha Families, Five
reality, nature of, 48–9, 188–97, 218–24. *See also* "as it is"
realization, 33. *See also* enlightenment
Realms, Six, 128, 131–48, 167
  —Animal, 131, 132, 140–1, 145
  —God, 131, 132, 143–5, 177. *See also* Deva Loka

Realms (*Continued*)
—Hell, 132–3, 138–9, 140, 146
—Human, 131, 132, 141–2, 145, 146
—Hungry Ghosts, 132, 139–40. *See also* Preta Loka
—Jealous Gods, 131–2, 142–3, 145. *See also* Asura Loka
Red Rock Jewel Valley, 45–6, 241
renunciation, living·quality of, 198–9, 240; as spiritual game, 41, 115–6, 163
rigidity, 157, 173–4. *See also* seriousness
rishi, 190
Rudra, 231

samadhi, 119, 133–4, 154–5, 176, 205–6. *See also* meditation
samadhi, vajra-like, 119, 181, 218
sambhogakaya, 231
samsara, circle of, 146, 159; nirvana in, 220–1, 232, 242. *See also* ego, development of
samsaric mind, 58; highest level of, 144
sangha, 26–7, 53
sanity, basic, 9–11, 47–8, 153
Sanskrit, 32, 55, 123, 151–2, 187, 197, 220
satori, 117–8. *See also* enlightenment, instant
security, mechanisms of, 5–6, 125–7, 56, 59–60, 91–2, 152, 211. *See also* ego, self-preservation quality of
self, the. *See* ego
self-acceptance, 28, 64, 160. *See also* "being as you are" *and* self-trust
self-consciousness, 5, 7, 42–3, 111, 143–4, 208; birth of, 123–5; in art, 238; and bodhisattva, 172. *See also* ego *and* self-watching
self-criticism, 24, 93, 132–3, 142–3
self-deception, 54–5, 63–75, 83, 91–7, 134
self-destruction, 20
self-luminous cognition, 194–6
self-trust, 20, 97–109. *See also* confidence
self-watching, 21–2, 59–60, 70–1, 73–5, 106, 111, 119, 125, 161, 169; transmuted by prajna, 178. *See also* ego *and* evaluation
seriousness as aspect of spiritual materialism, 14, 111–9, 154. *See also* rigidity
shamatha meditation. *See* meditations
Shantideva, 106, 175
Shariputra, 187–8
shelter, search for, 26–7, 125. *See also* security
shila, 100, 173–4. *See also* Paramitas, Six
shopping, spiritual. *See* eclecticism
shunyata, 187–206; death of, 217–9; experiencing of, 187, 190, 197, 201–2, 234; and form, 188–90, 196–9, 207–8; relative to samsara, 220–1; in Tantric thought, 217–21, 224, 231–2. *See also*

openness *and* space
simplicity, loss of, 14–5, 22, 124–5
Sitting Bull, 105
Skandhas, Five, 123–8, 151, 219–20. *See also* Realms, Six
—Concept, 127–8, 130
—Consciousness, 128, 130–1, 133, 145, 167
—Feeling, 126, 128, 130
—Ignorance-Form, 123–4, 133–4
—Perception-Impulse, 126–7, 128, 130
skillful means, 187, 210
soul, 193
space, dwelling upon, 143–4; fear of, 22, 69–70; solidification of, 122–6, 128–9, 133–4, 146–8; for communication, 157, 161–2, 180; in *mahavipashyana* meditation, 168–9; relative to form, 160–1
Speech, Lord of, 5–8. *See also* Materialism, Three Lords of
spiritual friend, necessity of, 83, 87–9; stages of meeting, 41–7; distinct from "guru", 39–40. *See also* guru
spiritual materialism, consequences of, 7–8; definition of, 3; escaping, 158–9; seduction of. 119
spiritual path. *See* dharma *and* meditation
spirituality, Buddhist overview of, 4–11
spontaneity of awakened state, 169; of bodhisattva action, 103, 182, 238; in communication, 162; and meditation, 10, 97
stupidity, impulse of, 127, 130; realm of, 140; distinct from ignorance, 125
struggle, absence of, 9, 11, 100–3; futility of, 23, 71–2; 135, 136; ironic character of, 112–5; maintaining ego by, 5, 86–7; as origin of suffering, 152–3
surrender, 238; necessity of spiritual friend for, 87–8; pain of, 81; and Bodhisattva Path, 99, 198; to guru, 23, 37–9, 82–5; of preconceptions, 23–8
suffering, origin of, 152–3, 195; realization of, 8, 119, 151–3, 159; truth of, 151–2, 162; truth of origin of, 151–3, 162. *See also* duhkha; pain; *and* Truths, Four Noble
symbolism. *See* iconography *and* perception

Tantra, 47, 217–43; categories of energy in, 224–30; iconography of, 223, 230–4; Lower, 222; practices of, 231–2; principle of transmutation in, 218–23, 230–241; transition from Mahayana to, 208, 218–9. *See also* Buddhism *and* Vajrayana
tathagata, 169–70
tathagata-garbha, 47. *See also* Buddhanature *and* intelligence, basic

tathata, 169–70, 191, 220. *See also* "as it is"

teacher. *See* guru *and* spiritual friend

techniques, spiritual, 22, 73, 160; falling away of, 197; insufficiency of, 160; strengthening ego by, 3, 7. *See also*: asceticism; disciplines, spiritual; gymnastics, mental

thamal-gyi-shepa, 59, 220. *See also* wisdom, ordinary

theism, 4, 191–2

thoughts, discursive: communication and, 162; meditation and, 10, 133, 151, 161, 167; as defense mechanism of ego, 10, 122, 197; origination of, 122–8, 151–3

thoughts, subconscious, 233

Tibet, Marpa and, 32–6; meditation of, 153–4; Trungpa Tulku and, 18–9, 53

Tibetan language, 32, 109, 187, 205, 220; lore, 5, 17, 43, 114–5, 121, 209; people, 79

Tilopa, 17, 33, 96–7, 221

transcendence, 172, 220. *See also* ego, transcendence of

transcendental discipline. *See* Paramitas, Six *and* shila

transcendental energy. *See* Paramitas, Six *and* virya

transcendental generosity. *See* dana *and* Paramitas, Six

transcendental knowledge. *See* Paramitas, Six *and* prajna

transcendental meditation. *See* dhyana *and* Paramitas, Six

transcendental patience. *See* kshanti *and* Paramitas, Six

transmutation, principle of. 178. *See also* Tantra

trishula, 231

Trungpa Tulku, 53

Truths, Four Noble, 119, 151–164
—First Noble Truth. *See* duhkha *and* suffering
—Second Noble Truth. *See* suffering, origin of
—Third Noble Truth. *See* goal, truth of *and* non-striving
—Fourth Noble Truth. *See* dharma *and* path, truth of

upaya, 212. *See also* skillful means

Vajra, 119. *See also* Buddha Families, Five

vajra, anger, 234

Vajrayana, 224, 239. *See also* Buddhism *and* Tantra

Vedantism, 191

vidya, 123–4. *See also* Skandhas, Five

Vidyadhara, 243

vipashyana meditation. *See* meditations

vipassana meditation. *See* meditations, vipashyana

virya, 100, 175–7. *See also* Paramitas, Six

"what is". *See* "as it is" *and* tathata

wisdom, crazy, 109, 210, 230, 243. *See also* jnana

wisdom, ordinary, 220. *See also* thamal-gyi-shepa

Wisdoms, Five, 229, 231; Mirror-like, 224–5; of All-Accomplishing Action, 228–9; of All-Encompassing Space, 229; of Discriminating Awareness, 226–7; of Equanimity, 223, 225. *See also* Buddha Families, Five

"working on oneself", excesses of, 94–6, 104; limits of, 63–4; necessity of individual, 77–8, 89

world. *See* reality

yana, 99; Three *Yanas*, 224

yeshe, 109. *See also* intelligence, primordial

yidams, 230–3

yoga, 7, 15, 94, 160

Yogachara school. *See* Buddhism

Zen, 48–9, 79, 80, 190, 232–3

Chögyam Trungpa (1940–1987) was widely admired as a meditation master, teacher, and artist. He was the author of many books on Buddhism and the path of meditation, including *The Myth of Freedom, Meditation in Action,* and *Shambhala: The Sacred Path of the Warrior.*

Trungpa Rinpoche was born in eastern Tibet. An incarnate lineage holder in the Kagyü and Nyingma school of Tibetan Buddhism, he was Supreme Abbot of the Surmang Monasteries, where he received, at the age of eighteen, the degree of Khyenpo (comparable to a doctorate in theology, philosophy, and psychology). As part of his education in Tibet, he also studied and practiced traditional arts such as calligraphy, poetry, dance, and *thangka* painting.

When the Chinese invaded Tibet in 1959, Chögyam Trungpa fled to India. There, by appointment by His Holiness the Dalai Lama, he served as spiritual advisor to the Young Lamas' Home School. In 1963 he traveled to England, where he attended Oxford University.

Trungpa Rinpoche was invited to teach in the United States in 1970. With his home in Boulder, Colorado, he traveled and taught extensively, establishing more than one hundred meditation centers in the United States, Canada, and Europe. The association of Vajradhatu that he founded in 1973, now called Shambhala International, coordinates the activities of these centers. Trungpa Rinpoche also founded the Naropa Institute, an innovative liberal arts college, and Shambhala Training.

Chögyam Trungpa moved to Halifax, Nova Scotia, in 1986. He died there the following year on April 4.

Information on any of the Shambhala centers may be obtained by contacting Shambhala International, 1084 Tower Road, Halifax, Nova Scotia, Canada, B3H 2Y5 (902-425-4275).

Shambhala Classics

Appreciate Your Life: The Essence of Zen Practice, by Taizan Maezumi Roshi.

The Art of War, by Sun Tzu. Translated by The Denma Translation Group.

The Art of Worldly Wisdom, by Baltasar Gracián. Translated by Joseph Jacobs.

The Book of Five Rings, by Miyamoto Musashi. Translated by Thomas Cleary.

The Book of Tea, by Kakuzo Okakura.

Kabbalah: The Way of the Jewish Mystic, by Perle Epstein.

Lovingkindness: The Revolutionary Art of Happiness, by Sharon Salzberg.

The Myth of Freedom and the Way of Meditation, by Chögyam Trungpa.

Narrow Road to the Interior and Other Writings, by Matsuo Bashō. Translated by Sam Hamill.

The Rumi Collection: An Anthology of Translations of MevlânaJalâluddin Rumi. Edited by Kabir Helminski.

Seeking the Heart of Wisdom: The Path of Insight Meditation, by Joseph Goldstein and Jack Kornfield.

Siddhartha, by Hermann Hesse. Translated by Sherab Chödzin Kohn.

Start Where You Are: A Guide to Compassionate Living, by Pema Chödrön.

T'ai Chi Classics. Translated with commentary by Waysun Liao.

The Tibetan Book of the Dead: The Great Liberation through Hearing in the Bardo. Translated with commentary by Francesca Fremantle and Chögyam Trungpa.

The Tree of Yoga, by B. K. S. Iyengar.

The Way of a Pilgrim and The Pilgrim Continues His Way. Translated by Olga Savin.

When Things Fall Apart: Heart Advice for Difficult Times, by Pema Chödrön.

The Wisdom of No Escape and the Path of Loving-Kindness, by Pema Chödrön.